Every Woman's Guide to Making Her Emotions
the Holiest Part of Her!

by
Carol McLeod

HARRISON HOUSE
TULSA, OKLAHOMA

Holy Estrogen!
Is lovingly dedicated to the women in my heart:

To the daughters that God gave to me after years of infertility who
are now my role models and best friends for life!

Carolyn Joy
and
Joni Rebecca

To my daughters-in-love who adore my sons
and have stolen my heart!

Emily Rose
Elizabeth Anne
and
Allie Meredith

To my two sweet granddaughters who light up my life
with little-girl joy and precious smiles!

Olivia Mae
and
Amelia Grace

To my dear mother-in-law who calls me higher by her example.

Margaret Rebecca Truelove Mcleod

And especially to my mom ... who has taught me
what it means to be a woman of God.

Joan Carol Burton Ormanoski

16 15 14 13 12   10 9 8 7 6 5 4 3 2 1

Holy Estrogen!
ISBN: 978-160683-398-8
Copyright © 2011 by Carol McLeod

Endorsements

Pastor Sharon Daugherty

Carol has such a unique way of driving home the truth while making you laugh. She is so on target with what God wants to say to today's women. She understands and gives insight as to how to overcome in life. This is a great reading!

Pastor Sharon Daugherty is Senior pastor at Victory Christian Center, Tulsa, Oklahoma

John Mason

Are you looking for more of Him and less of you? In her hilarious and encouraging book, *Holy Estrogen*, Carol McLeod opens up her life to show you how you can make your emotions the holiest part of you...REALLY! As a happily married man for more than thirty-four years, I'm recommending this book to every husband (and wife) I know.

John Mason is the author of numerous national bestselling books, including An Enemy Called Average.

Phil Cooke, Ph.D.

The thing I love about Carol Burton McLeod is originality, and she doesn't disappoint with her new book *Holy Estrogen*. It's serious, funny, and thought provoking, all at the same time.

This isn't just a women's book. It explores a mystery that baffles most men, and that's why it's not an exaggeration to say this book could save a lot of marriages.

Phil Cooke, Ph.D. is a filmmaker, media consultant, and author of Jolt! Get the Jump on a World that's Constantly Changing.

Michael Fletcher

Straight, faith-filled talk on some tough topics, this book will help you "take control" of your life and move to the next level!

Michael Fletcher is Senior Pastor Manna Church.

Lisa Osteen

Ladies, we all need help and encouragement when it comes to our emotions and I have never seen a book like *Holy Estrogen* that my friend Carol McLeod has written. Get ready to be encouraged, empowered, and changed forever! You are made for more than simply surviving life and Carol will show you how to live your life to the fullest.

Lisa Osteen is Associate Pastor Lakewood Church, Houston, TX, Author of several books including the latest, You Were Made for More.

Gloria Cotten

Hooray! Someone has finally written an honest, practical, Biblical book about the hormonal ebb and flow that shapes a woman's life. For most of us women, the words "holy" and "estrogen" would never be found in the same sentence! But Carol approaches the subject with sensitivity, humor, and wisdom. How wonderful to be reminded that God created estrogen! Carol's practical and candid suggestions for "how to make your emotions the holiest part of you" encourage women to see their femininity as a wonderful gift from God rather than a curse. I heartily recommend it to women of all ages and stages of life!

Gloria Cotten is the wife of Michael, mother to three grown sons, mother-in-law to three lovely women, and grandmother to seven boys and girls from ages 1 to 12. A popular speaker at women's conferences and church groups, she has written a book, In the Beginning, *published in 2001. She and Michael have served the Body of Christ together for over 30 years raising up churches, overseeing churches, preaching and teaching all over the US and abroad. They currently live in Fayetteville, NC.*

Michael Cotten

Let's start with the assumption that God knew what He was doing when He made women. Further, that He does not exist for just part of a woman's life, but for all of her. If we believe Satan, women are just TOO emotional, TOO controlled by their emotions and feelings and generally untrustworthy. That's a lie! God's work at creation is perfect, and He intends for every woman (and man) to be able to experience God in their emotions. "You can either be controlled by your emotions or you can allow the Holy Spirit to control your emotions." Carol's book will generate faith in you for yourself and your emotions.

CAUTION: This book is refreshingly direct. It will not pat you on the hand, but will confront old lies, stereotypes and fears.

Michael Cotten resides in Fayetteville, North Carolina, is married to the lovely Gloria and has three sons, three lovely daughters-in-law and seven brilliant grandchildren. He was trained as an attorney, but for the last 30 years has been on a sole retainer with God. He has raised up churches, traveled the world as a prophet, been the apostolic leader of

Grace Churches International and, with the lovely Gloria, leads Antioch International Ministries. Michael is also a co-leader of the International School of Prophetic Development and leads prophetic seminars and schools around the world. He and Gloria have been married for 43 years. He has written and published the first of a series of books on prophecy entitled, When God Speaks.

Gloria and Michael Cotten

How encouraging for both men and women to be reminded that God made estrogen! Surely God knew what He was doing! Carol has written a refreshingly direct but mercifully humorous book that confronts old stereotypes and releases fresh vision for femininity. Michael says: A few years ago, my constantly chilly wife tossed the covers off and announced, "I'm hot." We lowered the temperature, gave guests a comforter and I put on a sweater. This is godly compatibility! God is in control of everything, including hormonal fluctuations!We love this book and think you will too.

Ron McIntosh

Carol McLeod is a gifted minister and communicator to anyone, but especially to women. Beyond her giftings, Carol is an incredible person and an outstanding wife and mother. Her new book, *Holy Estrogen,* is a gem and speaks to the core issues that cause women to operate at their full capacity. She expertly shows people how to master their emotions so as believers, they can dictate to life, not have life dictate to them. Attitude is a mental conditioning that determines interpretation and response to your environment…it does determine altitude (in life). Master your emotions, master your life. Carol has found a profound, yet simple way to show that all of Christianity and life comes down to learning how to master the heart (Proverbs 4:23, 23:7). Proverbs 4:23 tells us to guard your heart, for out of it comes the issues of life. The term "issues" in Hebrew means boundaries. The boundaries of your life are determined by what is in your heart.

In your hands is a tool to master estrogen and your emotions in such a way to break the boundaries of your life. Wonderfully written in a heartfelt style, this book will cause women to go from "desperate housewives" to being distinctive women...and cause men to truly understand the love of their lives. This is a wonderful, impacting read.

Ron McIntosh is president of Ron McIntosh Ministries and I.M.P.A.C.T. (a church leadership group). He is executive director of Victory Bible Institute and author of four books.

Tamara Graff

Carol Mcleod understands what makes women tick. For years, she has studied, embraced and encouraged women and gained tremendous insight into their lives. *Holy Estrogen* is a delightful and practical guide to help women better understand themselves and God's plan for their fulfillment.

Tamara Graff is Co-Pastor of Faith Family Church Victoria, Texas.

Lynette Lewis

Carol McLeod "gets it" when it comes to women, emotions, and loving God. In her witty and wise style she shows all of us how to choose the life we were always meant to live!

Lynette Lewis is a corporate consultant, speaker and author of Climbing the Ladder in Stilettos.

Chris Alan Busch

Holy Estrogen? A paradox of terms to be sure. Or so I thought. Most men will glance at this title and surf on. That would be a mistake. As an experienced passenger on the hormonal roller coaster with my darling wife of nearly four decades, I found that Carol's book actually had a lot of juice for me. If you are a man and you've been foraging for a flake of hope or a nugget of understanding, take this book... and read it. And please allow me to say in advance, "You're welcome!"

Chris Alan Busch is founder and CEO of LightQuest Media, Inc.

Contents

Introduction 17

1-Desperate Housewives 25

2-A Matter of the Heart... 41

3-You Are Not Schizophrenic!.. 55

4-A Soul Out-of-Control... 69

5-One Defining Moment 87

6-The Big 3 99

7-The Problem with People 117

8-It's Time for a Change 131

9-The Blahs...145

10-Disappointments, Broken Hearts
    and Other Maladies of the Soul...................165

11-What Will Your Legacy Be? 187

12-Every Woman's Battle................................209

Acknowledgments

Oh! How I don't want to leave anyone out! This book is certainly the result of precious relationships too numerous to count!

Craig...thanks for putting up with my estrogen...holy and otherwise! Thanks for being my husband, the father of our great crew of children, an anointed pastor and leader and truly...my best friend.

Matthew...my first-born. I fear that you were the victim of more unholy estrogen moments than any of the others. Thanks for loving your mom in spite of it all. You define the word " excellence". I am so proud of the man, coach, husband and father that you are today. Your greatest win, on or off the court, is definitely Emily, Olivia and Wesley.

Christopher...the second son. Thanks for teaching our family how to sing and laugh. We are all cheering for you as you round this next corner of destiny! Thanks for giving Liz and Amelia Grace the last name "McLeod".

Jordan...the miraculous answer to our prayers. You have always been a living, breathing demonstration that God really does hear our prayers and that He is still in the miracle business today. Pa and Pappy would be so proud of you...so am I! Thanks for choosing Allie and for the dearest gift ever...Ian Wesley!

Joy-Belle...you are always in my heart. Three Squeezes. God has such wonderful surprises for you. I can't wait to see it all unfold. "A daughter is a little girl who grows up to be your best friend."

Joni Rebecca...oh no! You are going to leave me like the rest did! Know that Mama is always at home...praying and believing...and trying not to cry! Go for it, Joni! Pray big prayers because you serve a big God!

Mom and Leo...thanks for encouraging phone calls and Amish Bakery treats. Leo - thanks for loving us and accepting all of us like we were your very own. Mom - thanks for teaching me how to dream big dreams and serve a big God. We all love TEAM LEO!

Nanny...thanks for doing the laundry, sweeping floors and keeping us all fed while I worked on this book. I know that while you worked on my behalf...you were also praying on my behalf! I love being with you and am honored to be your daughter-in-law.

Kathy - Thanks for making my life so much more fun! Thanks for the great stories and the wisdom. I would be so boring without you... and I fear to think who you would be without me!! I have loved raising our children together, homeschooling together and now...we will enjoy all of those grandbabies together!

Monica, Angel, Susie, Keri, Lisa and Sarah - you are truly first-string on the Just Joy! team. Thank you for your time, your hearts and your friendship. This has been quite a ride and I have a feeling that we have only just begun! So...keep the key in the ignition and the pedal to the metal!

Debbie, Carol, Sandy, Marilyn and Patti - thank you for your support and your friendship. Thanks for doing grunt work, for wisdom and for prayer. I love doing life with each one of you! Thank you for helping me love and minister to the women of this generation. You are each pure gold in my book!

Loren, Janie, Jenna, Ashley and Avery - Friends who are family. What a gift you are to the McLeod's! We love laughing with you... dreaming with you...playing games with you...eating too much food with you...serving God with you...and changing the world with you!

Peter, Kelly, Sammy and Isaac - Thanks for finding room for two lonely parents in your hearts. Thanks for Sunday night suppers and a home that looks lived in again!

Diane, Karyn and Allison - Thanks for the love, support and prayers that come my way from Long Island! How I love you and Smithtown Gospel Tabernacle!

Christy, Anita, Diane and Cathy - God's got great things in store for His girls in Ohio! Talk about a divine appointment...you all were mine! I am blessed to call you my friends...truly sisters of the heart. I can't wait to come to the River again...and again...and again!

Dawn and Marilyn - Forever friends. How I miss you...still to this day. I love you and appreciate you forever. I am a better woman because of you.

Carolyn, Shannon and La-La - What did I ever do to deserve you?! Carolyn...my lifetime mentor. La-La...my lifetime sister. And Shannon...my lifetime little sis. Oh! That we lived next door! La-La would cook, clean and sing. Carolyn would keep us all sane and stable. And Shannon and I would dream and giggle.

John Mason - Who knew? Who knew that a college friendship could grow into powerful teamwork? You are a door-opener extraordinaire...a man who believes in someone else's dreams...and the greatest cheerleader of all time. I am so thankful that it is Linda's job to keep you in line.

Chris Busch, Jamie Gaylor and my dear friends at LightQuest Media - When I think about all of you, I think about how Paul and Silas sang at the midnight hour in prison. Their song of praise opened prison doors and shook the very foundations of that old Roman prison. Thanks for loving Jesus enough to open doors on my behalf. Thanks for shaking heaven and earth to make way for Defiant Joy! Radio. It is my honor indeed.

Julie Werner, Chris Ophus and the team at Harrison House - Thanks for taking a chance on me and my holy estrogen! I pray that we are all forever changed because of it!

And most importantly...my highest praise and symphony of worship is sung to my Savior and King! To Him Who has touched my life with His holiness and nothing has ever been the same!

Introduction

Estrogen! What is up with estrogen?! A medical dictionary boldly states that estrogen plays a significant role in a woman's mental health issues. Lovely…that's the problem with my mental health… it's estrogen!

A medical dictionary also patiently and wisely explains that a woman's levels of estrogen can cause mood lowering. H-m-m-m… mood lowering. I think that the words "mood" coupled with "lowering" may strike abnormal fear in the heart of every husband, child and co-worker alive today.

Let's read on in the medical dictionary: *Because of recent studies with lab rats, it is believed that estrogen levels may influence obsessive compulsive disorder.*

Lab rats? OCD? Estrogen? Me? All in the same sentence? How can I even be thought of in the same category as obsessive compulsive lab rats?!

How to Make Your Emotions the Holiest Part of You

Our emotions are compelling, dynamic determinants in our lives and as Spirit-filled women, we need to determine how to control their power. We also need to consider the scope of our emotions and finally, we need to govern their consequences. This is no easy task and just may take a lifetime to master. It's all a wonderful part of life this side of heaven.

That's what this book is about: how to make your emotions the holiest part of you. This book is a guide to enable every Christian woman to become less selfish and more like Christ. You can either be controlled by your emotions or you can allow the Holy Spirit to control your emotions. Is it really that simple? Well…yes and no. Yes, because the Holy Spirit really is that powerful. No, because if it were that simple, there would be no need for a book like this one! The solution is obvious – the problem is not with the Holy Spirit but with me.

What else is this book about? Women. At their finest, and at their worst. It is about women in all stages and phases of life who don't want to just act like Jesus but at their deepest level, they want to be like Jesus. If you are a woman, you have felt the devastating backlash of out-of-control emotions. Also, as a woman, you have certainly experienced the sweet delight and comfort of positive, godly emotions. And, unfortunately, as a woman you have most likely been painfully wounded by someone's anguish or distress.

Roller Coasters, Fruit and Hysteria

I do not believe that God intended for women to live a roller coaster life, ordered by the fluctuation of some hormone that they exert absolutely no control over. God's plan has always been that you would decrease and He would increase. God has an answer for every emotional outrage to which you feel entitled. It's called *fruit*, and boy, does it taste good! God's fruit will nourish and delight not only the person who accepts it, but also the world who is impacted by the fruitful and luscious life of the person who offers it.

In all of recorded history, the emotions of women have been characterized as unique from those of men. In ancient Egypt, as early as 1900 BC, there was a record of a condition called "hysteria." This condition, defined as "lack of control over emotions and behavior," was found chiefly in women and so was archaically blamed on "the wandering of the uterus."

When girls become women, generally around the ages of 12-14, there is a surge of hormones due to puberty as these young women enter a season in life in which they are able to reproduce. Not only are there physical changes attributed to this ever-increasing hormone, but there are emotional changes as well. What happened to that sweet little princess who sat on her daddy's lap and begged to help her mama with the dishes? She now thinks that her father is an embarrassment and her mother is a controlling shrew. What happened to her? Estrogen happened to her!

These hormones that are a gift and a necessity of maturity often result in a roller coaster of emotional fluctuation and physical change. We all know the exhilarating fright of ascending up one steep emotional incline filled with excitement about reaching new heights and the thrill of all that lies ahead, only to come crashing unexplainably, and sometimes violently, down.

How is a woman able to love so deeply and completely one moment and then find herself compelled to spew brutal, impetuous verbiage on the people she loves the very most? Is every woman an unappetizing goulash of schizophrenic emotions?

Valid Questions

You have seen the picture of this next woman mocked in the funny papers, talked about in sermons and used as an embarrassing illustration of all that is wrong with Christian women. "Wendy Worship" goes to church and sits as close to the front as she can with her handsome, but quiet, husband and 4 or 5 robotic but well-dressed progeny. She enthusiastically and loudly enters into worship singing, "Lord, You are good all the time!" Her spiritual heart is boldly placed on her lovely sleeve as she proclaims through corporate song, "I love to worship You...You are my strength when I am weak." But then, on the way home, she becomes disgusted with the behavior of her children and so she unleashes auditory manure upon their young and vulnerable hearts. Wendy is perturbed with the driving of her prince in shining armor and so she gives him the raw emotional rug burn of the silent treatment. Wendy's feelings were hurt that morning at church because the pastor's wife didn't look at her and thus, her attempts at spiritual correctness were largely ignored, so Wendy simmers in a raw, boiling cesspool of emotional sewage.

Do you bear any emotional twinship with "Wendy Worship"? Perhaps, like Wendy, you have asked yourself these questions due to emotional hurricanes for which you bear complete and utter responsibility:

Who am I?!
How can even God love me?!
Why does my husband tolerate me?
Have I eternally warped my children?

Once Upon a Fairy Tale

Married women are not the only sources of feminine outrage and picturesque testimonies to girls gone estrogen-wild. For those of you who are single whether in your 20's or 70's, you are mournfully familiar with the cold, empty loneliness that creeps into your heart because everyone is a lovely and complete duet and you are a solo act.

"Sanctified Susie Single" is always looking for prospects on the distant horizon and when a new single guy arrives at church, she is the first to check him out. There he is…in all his Christian hotness! The next week, Susie comes to church with her nails done, modeling a new fashionable, yet modest, designer outfit and smelling mighty fine. She had her roots done this week, not to mention the fact that she spent time in the gym every day and is down an impressive 3.5 pounds. But it is in her mind where the most significant changes have occurred, because Susie has concocted a fairy tale of desperate love at first sight and believes that Mr. No Name Christian just might be the infamous "the one"! This is her time to start planning nuptials like no other!

As Susie walks demurely into church looking for Mr. Possibility, her gaze meets his warm brown eyes across the sanctuary when, to her horror, she sees that he is surrounded by a petite wife and 6 adoring children! How could he do this to her? Suddenly single again, Susie refuses to worship but weeps and walks out before the sermon appropriately entitled, "Trusting God In All Seasons of Life!"

The Older but Wiser Girl

You may be well beyond the years of estrogen-laced instability and passion, but now find yourself dealing with loneliness and regret. Perhaps you long for the days when fairy tales were still a possibility and when a house, filled with the noise of family, was a blessing and not a nuisance. For the golden girls of Christianity, sighing has become an Olympic sport for which they could win a gold medal, and these girls are definitively positive that the best days are behind and not ahead.

During the latter years of one's life, it is easy to walk backwards through each day and look longingly toward the past. It is easy to plant a garden of "if-onlies" and to wallpaper every room of your life with regrets. These painful yearnings are the root of rabid depression during years that should be filled with the blessings of God.

Refute the Reputation

It's sadly true...we deserve the reputation that we have hung around our girlish necks. Women do indeed frequent the roller coaster of emotions more than men; we take so many more dips and turns than do our male, and more stable, counterparts. Statistics show that women are twice as likely to experience depression as men and that depression is the leading cause of disability for women in the entire world.

At your very worst, estrogen-induced moments, you think that what you want is to ventilate and violate. You think that if you pout and worry and groan and wail, that you will somehow feel tragically fulfilled. You think that brooding and simmering with discontent is what you deserve to do. You think that yelling at your kids, talking about your friends, withdrawing from your husband and being curt with your mom is your strategy for successful human living. When what you really need is to get over yourself and all of that! What you truly need, in the deepest part of you, is more of Christ and less of you.

You really do not desire to be "Wendy Worship" or "Sanctified Susie Single." Who you sincerely desire to be is a woman overflowing with joy and peace who has her heart set on producing a bumper crop of God's delicious fruit. God gave you estrogen so that you would be a woman who is fully alive on the inside and wholeheartedly engaged with the life that He has given to you. Your true heart's desire is to be a woman who is at her absolute finest when God is allowed to be all that He is inside of you! You will never be this person by focusing on your pain, your disappointment, your emotions or your estrogen. You will become this woman when the outrage is finally subdued and the personality of the Holy Spirit is lovingly fertilized in your heart.

1

Desperate Housewives

It's an incredible truth: You were strategically placed here, at this time in history, by God for His plans and purposes. He needed someone just like you to love the unlovable...to bring joy to a dark, cold world...to reveal peace in confusing conversations and situations...and to be kind at times when our culture is desolately cruel. God, the Creator of the Universe, needed someone just like you to be constantly optimistic in the face of frustrating circumstances...to hope when there was no reason for hope...and to show patience to obstinate and ornery people. Because God needed you, He created you to reveal His heart. The problem is, as His very own children, we have acquired too many genetic characteristics of the world and have forsaken the lavishly bestowed attributes of God, our loving Father. The problem is, we would rather have it our way than His way. The problem is, we would rather emote a selfish perspective on a situation than exhibit delightful and delicious fruit.

"For we are His workmanship, created in Christ Jesus for good works, which God prepared beforehand, that we should walk in them."

- Ephesians 2:10

We were created by God to reveal His heart during this singular moment in all of recorded time. We were created to do His good works but instead, we have decided to morph into an emotional counterfeit of who He intended for us to be. God created us because there was a lack of "Godness" on earth, and so He sent you and He sent me. God will only reveal Himself through us to the extent that we allow Him to fill every corner of our hearts and lives. The magnificent and heart-stopping truth is that you can have as much of God as you could possibly want! The question has never changed from the Garden of Eden until today, *How much of Him do you want?*

You can hardly study a Bible character who was strategically used by God without observing their confrontation with this eternal question, "How much of Him do you want?"

Job had to answer that question in the face of tribulation and great loss. He answered it with these words, *"I know that You can do all things, and that no purpose of Yours can be thwarted. I will ask You, and You instruct me"* (Job 42:2 & 4). In spite of his great pain and disappointment, Job wanted all of God that He could access.

It bears asking again, *How much of Him do you want?*

Esther had to answer that question when confronted with the cruelty of another human being and circumstances which she found desperately frightening. Esther called a fast when her life came crashing down around her and found power and strength in her decision to honor God, even during moments of crisis. Esther proclaimed with her actions that even if she died, she would never allow fear or worry to win a battle in her life. Esther was not content to live a life dictated by someone else's brutality or the fear factor of the day, but wanted all that God was able to demonstrate of His character.

Have you answered the question yet, *How much of Him do you want?*

And then there was Jonah, a man who ran from God in complete and utter rebellion. However, after God captured his attention while he was camping out in the belly of a great fish, Jonah admitted that running from God was a strategy for inevitable defeat. *"But I will sacrifice to You with the voice of thanksgiving. That which I have vowed I will pay. Salvation is from the LORD"* (Jonah 2:9). Jonah had joined the mighty choir of the voices of the ages who were willing to die to self and live for God's purposes and His purposes alone.

May I ask you again? *How much of Him do you want?*

It's All Up to God...or Is It?

Our lives are not our own, and yet God has given them into our hands. Go back and read that first sentence again: *Our lives are not our own, and yet God has given them into our hands.* It is one of those holy contradictions that causes us to look resolutely into the face of God with absolute wonder.

It's true...you are God's workmanship. You have been created in Christ Jesus for one purpose alone: for the good works that God planned specifically for you before the beginning of time. It is God's plan that you walk in the life that He has planned and prearranged for your advantage. But, the choice is still up to you. You really can either have it your way or have it God's way.

"My life is continually in my hand ..."

- Psalm 119:109

Although you belong to God because He created you and He pre-designed an incredible life for you, He has still placed the choice for that miraculous life in your hands. One of the most practical instances of where we choose God or choose self is in our emotional preferences and habits. You must give up your right to whine and pout and then wholeheartedly embrace the plan of God for your life, which is found in the fruit of the Spirit. You were created for good works and not for the works of the flesh or for the opinions of your emotions.

The good works that Christ planned for you before you were even born are so much more than reading a devotional book or listening to worship music. The good works that God had in mind when He thought of you were so glorious that He declared across the ages that you were His very own masterpiece. God has had His eye on you since the beginning of time to do something so extraordinary through your life that even the angels would stand back in wonder and long to do what you were created to do!

The Power of His Presence

You will only be the person that God created you to be when you receive the power that He has created for you to have. Let's just all admit it, we are sadly unable to rise above the selfish demands of our estrogen without the power of the Holy Spirit. I am such an estrogen-saturated female that all I can ever do on my own is think about me and the way that I feel. But you were not created for estrogen-saturation, you were created for fruit, for good works, for the Kingdom of God and for power!

"But you will receive power when the Holy Spirit has come upon you; and you shall be My witnesses both in Jerusalem, and in all Judea and Samaria, and even to the remotest part of the earth."

- Acts 1:8

There are two distinct phrases in this scripture that are life altering and will set you into your emotional destiny. *"You shall receive power,"* is perhaps the most exciting phrase in the entire New Testament. You shall receive power! You don't have to slug through life with your own strength! You don't have to be content with emotional sewage and generational baggage! You shall receive power! You will never take authority over your estrogen-induced hysteria until you receive the power of the Holy Spirit.

"...And you shall be My witnesses," is the second stirring promise in this well-known verse. Receiving the power of the Holy Spirit enables you to become who God has created you to be! You need God's power so that you become a witness of His nature at this time in history. *You shall receive power and you shall be!*

You will never become all that God intended for you to become until you receive His power. Jesus knew that we would not be able to live an abundant life on planet earth without the power of the Holy Spirit and so He provided that exact power. I find myself praying this prayer nearly every day and sometimes several times a day because I am such a desperate woman:

Holy Spirit, fill me with Your power! I want all that You have for me – I want Your gifts and Your fruit. I want Your power more than anything else today. If You want me to pray for miracles and for healing – I will do it, so count me in! I am not fussy or picky but I want everything that You have for me. I want patience and self-control in addition to peace and joy and love. I will take every single ounce of power that You are willing to throw my way.

And then...you wait.

The Power of the Wait

As a young girl, I was raised in a Christian home in the idyllic 60's and 70's. My parents faithfully took their three children to a traditional, denominational church every Sunday morning. My mom played the pipe organ and my dad taught the adult Sunday School class. We were the first ones there each week and then the last ones to leave. On Sunday evenings, however, we went to a powerful, Pentecostal church in a neighboring town.

One of my earliest childhood memories is what happened inside my childlike soul on those dynamic Sunday evenings. I remember LaVerne Hamm, the song leader, directing the lively congregation in singing, "Victory in Jesus!" One week, we sang the chorus of that rousing hymn 17 times. I know because LaVerne's daughter, Brenda, and I counted it with little check marks on the back of our bulletin. I still remember. I guess that LaVerne thought if we sang it long enough that we would finally get it...there really is *Victory in Jesus!*

I can still hear the rhythm of Brother Sam Davis as he clapped with a new syncopation every time we sang the next chorus. Some Christians have the gift of teaching while others have beautiful, expressive voices. Some people can teach the Word of God with power and others serve wholeheartedly. Brother Davis had the gift of rhythm and he expressed it through his hands.

But what I remember the most about those Sunday evenings that laid a solid foundation in my soul was the joy of lingering at the altar. I remember responding to every altar call from the time I was eight years old through my teenage years. Oh, I didn't go up to get saved again every Sunday night, but I went up because, even as a child I was aware of my need for the power. I wanted the power that "Victory in Jesus!" announced. I wanted the power that was in Brother Davis' heart and hands. I wanted the power of the Holy Spirit.

The altar was weekly lined with young people who responded to the Spirit of God in that old-time Pentecostal church. The pastor's preaching would generally be completed by 9:00 or 9:30, but the prayer service was only just beginning. I remember waiting at the altar and crying out to God until beyond 11:00 p.m. many school nights. Our family of five would then make the 30 minute trip home in blinding snowstorms, and there would be no complaining the next morning as we all roused ourselves at 6:30 a.m. to begin the school week. The reason that I never complained in the dark of a Monday morning was because I remembered the power of the altar!

One Sunday evening that I vividly remember was when I was eight years old. I shot up out of the wooden pew and nearly ran toward the altar as soon as Brother Brown invited those forward who desired the baptism of the Holy Spirit. A trio of potential energy kneeled shoulder to shoulder and lifted their young arms toward heaven's Source. I was sandwiched between my childhood friend, Brenda, and my older sister, Norma. Sister Brown came and laid her sweet hands on each one of us and as she did, we received the power that changed our lives forever. We lingered for hours that night and just basked in the victory, the joy and in the power. As families were rising to go home at the end of that early Spring day, Sister Brown took Brenda and I aside and spoke a word to our innocent hearts, "This experience will be what *keeps* you a Christian through your high school years. You will need this power when you go to college and as you raise your children. You can have this power every day, not just on Sunday nights."

I learned a significant lifetime lesson in that little Pentecostal church over half my lifetime ago, *"There is power in the wait!"*

Impatient, Powerless Americans

"Gathering them together, He commanded them not to leave Jerusalem, but to wait for what the Father had promised, 'Which,' He said, 'you heard of from Me; for John baptized with water, but you will be baptized with the Holy Spirit not many days from now.'"

- Acts 1:4 & 5

Do not ever underestimate the power that you will find in the wait. I believe the reason that so many of us experience out of control emotions is that we no longer wait for what God has for us.

As American Christians, we have been so influenced by our culture that the wait is no longer a place of power but a place of emotion and frustration. We go to fast food drive-thrus to order a junk food meal for our family on the run. If we do have time to eat at home, we put our delivered pizza in the microwave so that it heats up more quickly. We go to the mall to get our nails done and then ask for a coat of quick-dry spray on our nails so we don't have to wait under the lights.

Teenage girls hate to wait to grow up. When they are eight, they dress like they are 12 and when they are 12, they dress like they are 16. Who is buying these young women the inappropriate clothes that they are wearing? Their mothers are using their credit cards to pay for what they can't wait to afford because they can't wait for their daughters to grow up!

Young men and women can't wait for marriage to enjoy the benefits thereof, and so they proceed with their own passions and desires. Your flesh categorically hates to wait and therefore, it has absolutely no desire to wait. Your flesh loves to demand its own way and then enjoy instant gratification. The favorite word of your flesh is "NOW!" Your flesh screams, "I want to say it *now* because I feel it *now* so I should have it *now* so I can do it *now!*"

When your flesh cries out, "Now!", God patiently responds, "No."

Waiting takes great discipline, which desperately needs to be developed in our children and in us because it is a virtue that will add great value to all of our lives. If your heart's desire is to be a powerful woman who has control over her emotions, then you must learn to wait in the presence of God for all that He has for you.

The Posture of the Wait

The disciples were involved in a strategic, life-changing activity while they waited for the power. Please understand that mere waiting does not complete the work when it comes to dealing with emotional outrage, misdirected passions and impatient desires. The frustration that comes from waiting only will be negated by adding a key ingredient to this equation, whose sum and substance is power.

"These all with one mind were continually devoting themselves to prayer, along with all the women."
                                                                    - Acts 1:14.

I truly do not have any magic answers for your estrogen-saturated issues, but I do have some insight into the Word of God for you. If you desire power to overcome and if you long for the ability to become who God created you to be, then you will first ask for His power. After you ask for the power, you will wait for the power. While you are waiting, you will continually devote yourself to prayer.

The compelling reason why the disciples were content to patiently devote themselves to prayer during the wait is because they knew that prayer changes the people who are doing the praying!

Prayer changes me. I am a better person when I pray. My family likes me better when I pray while I wait. When I pray, I make wiser decisions and am a nicer, kinder version of myself. Perhaps the reason you don't like yourself during moments of emotional outrage is because you have not experienced the power or the posture of the wait. The most powerful people I know are men and women of God who love to wait on their knees. Kneeling is not a foreign, difficult position for these history changing people because they understand that people who actually pray are the beneficiaries of heaven's power in their everyday lives.

Give Me Drugs!

I was about to become a mother for the very first time! It was only a few days past my given due date, but my doctor, who was also a family friend, was about to go out of town to a medical conference, and so I was given the drugs that were designed to induce my labor. Craig and I had taken childbirth classes and so we considered ourselves fully prepared for the adventure that was about to take place. We were taught in the classes not to refer to the process as "labor pains" but rather to use the politically correct term, "contractions." The woman who taught the childbirth class to the six couples who were preparing for the arrival of their babies, would forcefully correct each of us whenever we brought up the issue of pain. *It is not pain...it is a contraction.*

The contractions started slowly and I was in full control. I thoughtfully wrote my maternal ponderings in a beautiful journal that one of my friends had blessed me with at our baby shower. I fixed my lipstick every 30 minutes, because I wanted to look good in those post-birthing pictures.

After about 3-4 hours of insignificant, gentle progress, the doctor walked into our labor room. Craig and I both loved this dear friend who had guided us through the months of nausea and bloating; through backaches and heartburn. We had selected this doctor because he was a member of the church at which Craig was on staff. We knew in our novice hearts that we could trust this man of God to see us safely through to the delivery of our bundle from heaven.

As Chip, our doctor, examined me, he inconsequentially said, "I think that I will break your water to move things along." We smiled and laughed during this painless procedure and then Chip patted my hand as he walked out of the room.

The instant that Chip walked out of our birthing room, I was engulfed in red hot, searing pain! Who did he think he was? He has the nerve to call himself my friend?! I threw my journal at the door, thinking to myself, *Take that! You wanna-be man of God!*

I threw my lipstick at Craig and screamed, "These are not contractions! This is PAIN! That woman lied to me!"

After about five hours of relentless, horrific spasms, I looked at my nurse and declared, "When I am not in labor, I am a very nice person! I promise!"

After that pitiful outburst, the nurse initiated the process to have an epidural administered to my weary body. Within seconds, I returned to my normal, sweet self as I smiled after every push and laughed at my doctor's jokes. I even stopped screaming near profanities at my handsome, loving husband.

God made a way for you to be the very best version of yourself, even in life's worst moments. It's the epidural miracle cure of prayer!

If you will choose to continually devote yourself to prayer, you, too, will find relief from the onslaught of life's painful moments. Your emotions are strong and relentless and without prayer, you will lose control. Life's horrific spasms may be described as red hot and searing and the relief will only come as you continuously devote yourself to prayer.

The Strength of the Wait

"Wait for the LORD; be strong and let your heart take courage; yes, wait for the LORD."

- Psalm 27:14

There is a strengthening process that happens while you wait. Just as lifting weights strengthens your arms and chest, waiting strengthens your soul. Just as doing sit-ups strengthens your abdominal muscles, waiting strengthens you from the inside out. We mistakenly believe that the strongest response possible is to speak our minds or to fix a situation with our opinions. We wrongly assume that buying something or eating something will assuage our pain, but it is waiting and praying that will develop the unseen muscular structure of your soul.

Let me challenge you, the next time that you feel impatient and believe that you will just burst if you don't insert your opinion…wait. The next time that you are angry and feel the nearly uncontrollable impulse to verbally vomit over the object of your anger…wait. Perhaps a powerful habit for you to develop would be that before you speak anything in impatience or anger, you choose to write it down and pray over it. Maybe before you ever again give anyone a piece of your mind or demand your own way, you might consider pressing the emotional "pause" button and then take a prayerful step back. Allow me to suggest that prior to speaking anything potentially harmful, you might want to breathe deeply and give the matter to the Lord. All of those strategies involve waiting and then praying. You will be a stronger woman because of your powerful choice to wait and then pray.

There is a strengthening process that happens while you wait and you will miraculously discover that your heart will morph from being weak and filled with self, to being strong and filled with God and all that He is! It is a Biblical guarantee that when you ask for the power of the Holy Spirit, when you cultivate the virtue of waiting and then drug yourself with prayer, you will be a champion among Christian women alive on the earth today!

If situations or events cause an eruption of impatience to well up inside of your heart, take yourself through the three-step process again:

1 – Pray for power!
2 – Wait for strength.
3 – Pray for more of God and less of you.

Desperate Housewives

There is something about the heart of God that just loves desperate women who are thrust into His arms when their circumstances and relationships are spiraling out of control. We sadly hold ourselves back from His welcoming arms, believing that He will be frustrated with us or disappointed in us. But I can tell you that the Father loves a girl who is wise enough to declare, *"Jesus! Take control of me! Help me to love beyond my human capacity! I need more of You and less of me!"*

Why do we allow our very understandable humanity to keep us away from God's powerful and strengthening presence? When you are at your very weakest emotionally is the exact moment that you need to fling yourself into His arms and cry, *"Remind me, Lord, that I don't always get my own way or even want my own way! I want Your way on Your timetable!"*

I love the specific details that the Holy Spirit inserts into significant verses in the Bible. One of my favorite lines is in a scripture that we have already studied:

"These all with one mind were continually devoting themselves to prayer, along with the women."

- Acts 1:14

There is just something about the heart of a woman that demands prayer in order to be like Jesus. Do not ever underestimate the importance of the time that you spend daily on your knees, which will surely enable you to overcome your out-of-control emotions. Emotions are willful, youthful and sometimes violent and one of the most powerful forces in controlling a woman's emotions is knee-time. If you think that watching Oprah, reading *Good Housekeeping* magazine or going shopping are going to cure you of your emotional pain, then you are sadly deceived. The healing that takes place in a human soul while the body is in a position of prayer is eternal and miraculous. I cannot be like Jesus without time spent in His presence on my knees.

I can "act" like Jesus without prayer. I can win an Academy Award for smiling sweetly and reciting kind platitudes while my heart is roaring and my mind is vengeful. Although I know how to say the proper words, you might want to notice the smoke coming out of my double-pierced ears! Jesus does not desire for me to merely *act* like Him, but He longs for me to be like Him, and there is a decided difference. The difference takes place when I wait and when I pray because it is then that He becomes Lord of my emotions and of my thought life.

Women need to continually devote themselves to prayer in order to receive the power of the Holy Spirit and to strengthen their emotional resolve. I'm in…how about you?

A Matter of
the Heart

Your emotions travel 80,000 times faster than your thoughts travel. Isn't that amazing? This one piece of incredible information helps us to understand why when something bad happens, we feel raw and treacherous emotions, but we are not able to immediately remember what to do or who to call. Conversely, it is also true when something wonderful happens and we are wrapped up in the thrill of emotional exhilaration, at that moment also, we do not have the cognitive capacity to decide exactly what to do next. All reasonable and practical thinking arrives in our nerve center long after the emotion has expressed itself.

The tremendous speed of our emotional responses to life helps to explain why, even Christian women often tend to operate out of feelings rather than out of principle. Something...or Someone... needs to harness your emotions that travel at breakneck speed and force them to submit to the fruit that is only found in the Holy Spirit. If you continue to allow your emotions to rapidly yank you through life, you will always say things that are embarrassing, act in ways that are unbecoming, and never be the person that God intended for you to be. You will end up having the effect of a rapid-moving, volcanic eruption that decimates everyone in its violent, angry path.

Emotional Influencers

There are many issues that have crafted the emotional woman you are today. When you are able to understand your emotional history, it may become more apparent how to overcome each cause that has impacted your heart. Although there are many other influencers beyond the ones that are listed below, these are among the most powerful and prevalent.

How You Were Raised – Your childhood home had an emotional thermostat, which may determine many of your emotional choices as an adult. If your mother yelled often and loudly at the children and lived in constant frustration with her marriage, you may have a very low boiling point and minor things in life may cause you to erupt. Perhaps in your childhood home, little emotion was exhibited, including affection or encouragement, and so you are easily capable of freezing others out of your heart.

Nancy is a dear friend of mine who, although raised in a Christian home, understands as an adult that it was not an emotionally healthy home. Nancy's mother was the children's pastor at the mega-church they attended, so she spent large amounts of hours serving the church and the Body of Christ. But when Nancy's mother was at home, she yelled for little or no reason and was even known to throw objects at her children. Nancy was an extremely rebellious young adult because she knew that she could never please her mother, so why even try? Nancy's mother's emotional outrage had chased Nancy into rebellion.

After college, Nancy came back to the Lord and has raised her children in a home filled with love and joy. Rather than becoming like her mother, Nancy has taken great care to overcome the emotional temperature of her girlhood home. Now, when Nancy enters into a teaching moment with her two teenage girls, she is poignantly reminded of the distant screams in her past and the peace of her present.

Ethnic Background – We all have a reputation, don't we? The Italians and Irish are known to be overly emotive and to demonstrate great extremes with their feelings. Those with a Scandinavian or German heritage have the reputation of covering or hiding their emotions.

My maternal grandmother was a little Irish nurse who could dance a jig or tell you off quicker than you could whistle "Oh, Danny Boy"! Her mind was full of fire and truth and her heart was filled with love and laughter. But, her tongue was out of control! If she thought it, she said it, by golly! And she would always defend herself by saying, "It's the Irish in me!"

Christian women who are filled with the incredible Holy Spirit should never use their ethnic background as an excuse for emotions gone wild. As it says in Galatians 3:28, *"There is neither Jew nor Greek, there is neither slave nor free man, there is neither male nor female, for you are all one in Christ Jesus."*

Our identity in Christ overpowers all other identifications that we use to excuse emotional outrage. Your identity as a Christian should hold greater sway over your emotions than do your gender, your ethnic background or the color of your hair!

Rejection - If you felt the sting of rejection at an early age, before your self-esteem had been solidified, it has the capacity to strongly undermine your emotional stability.

Marilyn was just a little girl when her father left her mother and three siblings to live with his mistress and her children from her first marriage. Marilyn, her siblings and her mother prayed for nearly a decade before their daddy returned. This family enjoyed a miraculous reconciliation and the errant husband became a wonderful husband, daddy and grandfather in the last years of his life.

However, Marilyn, who is now in her 70's, has encountered a ferocious battle with fear and worry her entire life. The rejection that was thrust upon her as a little girl at the hands of her father impacted her ability to process the normal issues of life.

"Having predestined us to adoption as sons by Jesus Christ to Himself, according to the good pleasure of His will, to the praise of the glory of His grace, by which He made us accepted in the Beloved."
- Ephesians 1:5-6 (NKJV)

There is an acceptance that conquers all issues of rejection: Jesus Christ loves you and accepts you! He is crazy with delight over you and is head over heels in love with you! The most powerful Man in all of eternity longs to have a romance with you. You should never again deal with issues of rejection, knowing the sweetness of His embrace. Rest there.

Abuse Suffered – If you were abused either physically, verbally or sexually as a child or as a young adult, these horrific experiences, understandably, have the potential to cripple you emotionally. If you were abused at any significant juncture in your life, you know the reality of making decisions out of pain and mental anguish rather than out of principle. Women who were abused in the formative years of their lives often are unable to function with clear, mental processing but only out of an invisible, yet apparent, wound.

My heartfelt prayer is that these words will bring a measure of comfort to your mutilated soul: Jesus wept when you wept. Your pain was not your own, but was His pain as well. He was with you in the valley of abuse and longs to lead you out of it today so that you are able to function with His grace and with His peace. If you have not seen a Christian counselor yet, please do. Many women who have experienced the torture of abuse as a little girl have also found great healing in the power of prayer. Please ask one or two of your closest friends to pray for you today.

"Is anyone among you suffering? Let him pray."
- James 5:13 (NKJV)

"For just as the sufferings of Christ are ours in abundance,
so also our comfort is abundant through Christ."
- 2 Corinthians 1:5

How You Have Fed Your Soul - The emotional choices that we make daily have more impact than most of us are willing to admit. Our seemingly insignificant choices greatly impact our emotional stability every day of our lives. If you spend more time watching soap operas than you do reading the Word of God, then your life may take on the dramatic appearance of a soap opera. If you read more romance novels than you do devotionals, you will have an extremely difficult time controlling your heart and your emotions. If you listen to inappropriate music or go to seductive movies, then your insatiable soul will always scream for more. Each one of us will face an emotional crossroads when we must individually take responsibility for the woman that we are today. Now is that time for you.

What in your life do you need to clean out so that you can become the powerful woman God intended for you to be? What habits do you need to change so that you can lose the excessive emotional weight that you are disproportionately carrying throughout life? Your choices do indeed make a powerful and lifelong difference. Remember the words of Psalm 119:109, *"My life is continually in my hand...."*

Friends - My father always used to say to me, "Show me your friends and I will show you your future." As a teenager, I was unable to understand his wisdom and vehemently disagreed with this principle. However, as the years have passed and I have observed the seasons in my life, I would love the chance to say to my dad, *"You were right! You were so right, Daddy!"*

As women of God, we can be kind to everyone and minister to anyone, however, the friends that we welcome into the intimacy of personal relationship must be chosen wisely. If you have chosen friendships with women who are critical and angry, you are in grave danger of becoming like them. If you have entered into relationships with women who gossip and rehearse past wrongs, I can assure you that gossip is a highly contagious disease of the soul. If your friends are critical of their husbands, you will soon begin to wonder why you said, "I do," to Mr. Imperfection as well.

Because an emotion travels 80,000 times faster than a thought and therefore is able to reach your processing center in record-breaking time, when you are joined with the heart of someone who is easily upset and extremely critical, you will not be able to think your way out of it. You will feel what they feel and become who they have become.

The Heart of the Matter

"Watch over your heart with all diligence, for from it flow the springs of life."

- Proverbs 4:23

This familiar verse reminds Christians of every generation that there is little in life that is of more importance than securing control of your heart issues. Everything else that you do in life is impacted by how well you have guarded your heart, by all that you have allowed into your heart and by that which has then careened out of your heart.

When the word "heart" is used, particularly in the Old Testament, it refers to one's soul or the birthplace of the senses, emotions and affections. Your heart determines how you will act in any situation and is the seat of your will and purpose in life. The Bible says to "guard" or to "watch over" that part of your life with utmost attention.

If your best friend asked you to watch over their two year old, would you let him out of your sight? Would you allow that child to play in the street or to experiment with cleaning supplies? Absolutely not! You would watch over this little bundle of boundless energy with all diligence! We must use that same eagle-eyed diligence to guard the issues of your heart. This verse compels us to diligently set boundaries for what we allow our hearts to embrace and then to express. When our heart expresses the smallest amount of uncontrolled anger or other inappropriate emotion, you need to harness it and bring it back under control. Your heart or soul is the two year old of your emotional make-up and you must treat it like a two year old - *with all diligence!*

It is much easier to bring unbecoming emotions back from a mere two steps out of line than it is to corral them when they are easily recognized as being on the verge of sinful behavior. I have learned that it is much wiser to keep my emotions on a very short rope than it is to give them free rein on a daily basis.

If I were to ask you to keep my heirloom diamond ring while I was traveling out of the country, would you throw it in the trash? Would you loan it to someone else? Would you work in the muddy garden with it on your finger? Those are all absurdities and yet we treat our heart in much the same manner. We expose our hearts to matters and issues that will leave a residue of sin upon it; we give our heart easily away to people and causes that do not value the treasure that it is. Your heart is of great value to God and it should be treated as a treasure of great worth.

The problem is with the heart itself: your heart does not want to be guarded. It desires to loudly express itself and all of its opinions. Your heart is passionate about ventilating, vomiting and vocalizing every little feeling it has ever experienced. The Bible never says that we are allowed to express everything that is in our heart...it simply says to guard it.

The Hebrew language is rich in substance and often one word can have several different meanings. One of the aspects about Ancient Hebrew that I have grown to love is that words cannot just be defined by other words, but only by examining the picture that each word paints. The word "guard" is an example of such a word that becomes a masterpiece when you realize what it means from the Ancient Hebrew.

The first word picture that is exhibited by the word "guard" is a scene of ships coming into their home port during the time of war. The guard ships travel back and forth diligently in front of a huge territory that is actually much larger than the exact territory that requires homeland security. The guard ships are given one solitary, yet greatly significant command: *Do not allow any enemy ships even close to the home port.*

You are the navigator of the guard ships that are patrolling the waters around your heart and you must diligently blockade a huge expanse of emotional territory against the schemes of the enemy. This is especially true during times of war. When your circumstances are threatening to weaken you or cause you to be distracted, that is the moment when your heart needs guarding the very most. It is imperative that you use the Word of God as a high-powered weapon that fights off the thoughts or emotions with which the enemy is trying to wound you. This is also the most crucial time for you to enlist the power of the Holy Spirit and ask for His prowess in building an impenetrable barrier that will help guard your emotional responses to the battle.

The second word picture that is used in illustrating the meaning of the word "guard" is that of a watchman who never sleeps. Only expert and well-trained watchmen would know how to discern the slightest possible movement of enemy troops and be able to look for the subtleties of an enemy in camouflage. You are that watchman and you must be diligent to watch for any unwelcome emotions that are threatening your stability. The watchman that this word pictures is ready to shoot at the enemy when detecting the slightest, nearly unseen movement toward the city wall. You, too, need to be ready to shoot down all marauding, invading and uninvited emotions in your life.

The third, yet just as important, meaning of the word "guard" is not an illustrative meaning but a call to a particular lifestyle that not many are bold enough to embrace. The word "guard," in its fullest sense, also means to "guard with fidelity." The Holy Spirit instructs us to accept the standard of the United States Marine Corps and to embrace as our emotional motto, *Semper Fidelis*, which means "always faithful." We must be always faithful in refusing to embrace or express emotional outrage and pollution. We must be ever watchful during every season in our life and reject emotions that threaten to choke our ability to exhibit the fruit of the Holy Spirit.

The Word of God knows what is best for you and is offering instructions that are sure to lead into a life of abundance and emotional health. Guard your heart...there may be no greater key to emotional stability than this eternal word of advice from heaven's heart to yours.

An Emotional Security System

Guarding your heart is the most critical habit you will ever develop if your desire is to be an emotionally healthy woman. Nothing is of as great emotional importance as this one imperative from the Bible, *"Watch over your heart with all diligence, for from it flow the springs of life"* (Proverbs 4:23).

We mistakenly believe that guarding the family fortune is of the utmost importance and so we hire reputable and expensive lawyers to make sure that what is of temporary value is handed down from generation to generation. We spend thousands of dollars on security systems that guard our homes, our computers, our jewels and the family dog. However, the Bible tells us that the most important possession that you will ever have the opportunity to protect is your heart.

Several years ago, Craig and I were house hunting and truthfully, did not have the financial resources to buy the type of home that we were hoping to purchase. Our realtor and I traipsed through house after house that was in our price range but none of them were what we were looking for. My list of requests was simple: I wanted a house with a big yard and with a home office for Craig (so he could keep his mess in one room!). I was also hoping that we could find a home with four bedrooms and with a room that would accommodate our grand piano. We had been given the piano for our daughter, Joy, who is now in college as a piano major. I could not bear the thought of having to sell the piano and thus disappoint our talented and passionate daughter.

We were diligent in the hunt, but finally the day came when I realized that I was going to have to ease up on my list of requirements. I called our realtor, Jay, with the disheartening news and he said that he would draw up a new list of homes in a lower price range. However, only 15 minutes later he called me with great expectation in his voice and told me to meet him at 12 Lakeview Drive. I was there in record time and as I looked at the home, I thought to myself, *There is no way! I told him to go down in price...not up!*

Jay jumped out of his car and approached my car with a spring in his step, "Carol...this may be your house. It has a big yard, a home office, four bedrooms and a formal living room where you could place your piano. The seller wants out quickly because he owns another house and can't afford two mortgage payments. You could move in in two weeks!"

Jay and I both ran, not walked, to the front door and let ourselves in the gracious and stately home that was at the top of our price range. The next day, when Jay delivered the offer that was much lower than the asking price, the seller accepted it and threw in all of the appliances to boot!

We knew that some of the extra expenses that this house would require would take us out of our monthly budget. So, the first thing that we decided to cancel was the monthly fee paid to a security company for the alarm system.

When Craig made the phone call to the company, of course, they tried to talk him into keeping the safety service and offered all sorts of bells and whistles…literally. Craig kept kindly insisting that we were not able to afford the security service. At the end of the conversation, when the relentless salesperson knew that she had hit that infamous wall, she inserted one last thought, "Pastor McLeod, if you would just like to pay a yearly fee of $25, we will keep our signs in your yard so that anyone driving through your neighborhood believes that you are covered."

Well, that was an easy, "YES!" The purpose of the signs in the yard was to convince would-be robbers that our house had an alarm system so they should not waste their time trying to break in our Fort Knox home. We still have that security system sign in our yard and, nearly five years later, every time I drive into our yard, I think to my very secure self, *Yep! We got them fooled! No one is breaking in this house!*

Do you have the sign in the yard of your life? Do you have the principles found in the Word of God front and center in every decision you make, every word that you speak and every action you take? You better display the Word so that Satan knows not to waste his time trying to rob you of your joy and peace. The Word of God will scare away that scumbag Satan who tries to steal from Christians. Satan is on the prowl and one of the main valuables that he is trying to steal from you is your emotional stability. The Word of God puts a security system on your life that he will never be able to penetrate!

Satan wants to determine the quality of your life and so he is after your emotions. Put the sign in the yard of your heart that boldly declares, "Guarded and Protected by the Word of God!"

Why is your heart of such vital importance to the quality of your life? Why do you have to call in the Marines, act like a watchman who never sleeps and be on relentless patrol in the waters around your heart? This verse from Proverbs actually answers your question:

"Watch over your heart with all diligence, for from it flow the springs of life."

- Proverbs 4:23

Your heart, which is the birthplace of your emotions, has the final say in how you choose to live your life. Your heart determines what comes in to your life and what you allow out of your mouth and heart. Your heart determines how you act during anger and fear. Your heart has been given the responsibility to decide if your life will be like fresh, life-giving water or like a putrid, stagnant swamp. Your heart, truly, affects every other area of your life. Are you guarding it?

You Are <u>Not</u> Schizophrenic!

I love my little brother who is four and a half years younger than I am. He is an extremely successful businessman, a leader in his church and the father of four terrific young adults. Even though he now travels the continent, wheeling and dealing with top level corporate executives, I still see the remnant of the little boy I used to adore when I playfully call him, "Stevie."

I was often placed in charge of this bundle of perpetual energy when Mom and Dad would leave the home for the evening. Steve and I always got along famously and enjoyed every moment in each other's company. I would play Monopoly with him and always let him win so he would feel successful. (I guess that he can thank me for his business acumen today!) I always agreed to watch his favorite programs on television and spoiled him with milkshakes and pop-corn to his childlike heart's content.

He was the picture of younger brother perfection...until I asked him to do something that his little boy heart did not want to do.

"Stevie…it's time to go brush your teeth."

"No!" was his emphatic and ornery response to his adoring, older sister.

"Stevie .. it's time to put your toys away now."

"No!" he declared, even louder and with childish opinion.

"Stevie…you need to go to bed before Mom and Dad get home."

Suddenly, this cherub would cross his short arms, stomp his eight-year-old feet, screw up his formerly cute freckled face and assert with every ounce of resistance he could muster, *"I don't gotta if I don't wanna!"*

Oh…go ahead and laugh at the picture that I have just verbally painted. Laugh and laugh and laugh. In case you did not realize it, I actually just described you! When you demand your own way emotionally and refuse to guard your heart or your mouth, you, too, are displaying a childish picture of emotions gone wild. You might be one of those event-driven Christians who loves the Lord when your circumstances reveal a little white picket fence gloriously surrounded with the appropriate flower of the season. However, when God asks you to do something difficult such as love a fractious person or show patience when others are cruel, you become the very worst version of yourself, look God in the face and boldly profess, *"I don't gotta if I don't wanna!"*

A Soul Out-Of-Control

Let me tell you right now – what is coming up is my favorite part of the entire book! You have to read this next section in order to tackle your emotional instability and then to understand why even you don't understand yourself sometimes. If you are a smart woman, you will underline the highlights and then hand it to your husband, your mother and your best girlfriend so they, too, will have their "Aha!" moment of the heart.

I know that one of my life's messages is to help women deal with their emotions according to the Word of God. I pray that God will make the words jump off the pages and nestle deeply in your heart as you read this chapter.

You have a soul and you have a spirit. Both the soul and the spirit have been given to you by God and are part of your inner make-up which enables you to live an abundant life and to be a reflection of God's glory and character. However, when each of the two parts, the soul and the spirit, is not operating within their God-given mandate, it is then that women lose control of their emotions and melt into a puddle of only feeling with no fruit to offer.

Your spirit is the higher part of your inner person and your soul is lower. The spirit is the life principle bestowed upon man by God and is the part of you that perceives and grasps eternal things. You would never walk by faith and not by sight if you did not have a spirit. Your spirit was made to walk by faith and your soul only has the capacity of walking by sight.

"The spirit of man [the factor in human personality which proceeds immediately from God] is the lamp of the Lord, searching all his innermost parts."

- Proverbs 20:27 (AMP)

Your spirit is the part of you upon which the Spirit of God exerts influence and your spirit is also the receiver for hearing the voice of God. Martin Luther said, *"The spirit is the highest and noblest part of man which qualifies him to lay hold of incomprehensible, eternal, invisible things."*

Your soul, on the other hand, is the seat of your personality, your feelings, desires, affections and aversions. Quite simply, your soul is the birthplace of the entire spectrum of human emotion.

When the Bible references your soul, it is referencing that which influences your emotional responses to life.

In Luke 12, Jesus told a story about a rich farmer who was extremely successful and productive. When this prosperous farmer ran out of room to store his crops because the harvest was so bountiful, he decided to tear down his inadequate barns and build larger, more expensive ones. This man was so outrageously happy about his good fortune that he spoke to his soul and said, *"Soul, you have many goods laid up for many years to come; take your ease, eat, drink and be merry"* (v. 19).

God heard this pompous man's plans and was sadly disappointed with his decision to live a life of merely material productivity without a thought toward eternity. The farmer, whose soul was filled with mirth and barns were filled with plenty, had a spirit that was empty and dead.

"But God said to him, 'You fool! This very night your soul is required of you; and now who will own what you have prepared?' So is the man who stores up treasure for himself, and is not rich toward God" (vv. 20-21).

Our emotions will always chant, *If it feels good, do it! If you feel it, express it! You deserve to say everything you think, feel and believe!*

Many Christians make the very same mistake as did our affluent farmer friend in the parable of Jesus. We continuously feed our soul and ration the nutrition of our spirit. If you spend your life focusing on earthly pleasures and emotional desires, then your soul will grow out of control. Allow me to ask you an extremely appropriate and telling question as we deal with our out-of-control emotions, *Which is the healthier and stronger part of you? Your soul? Or your spirit?* For every Christian, the obvious and passionate answer should be, *"My spirit!"*

There is nothing intrinsically wrong with feeding your soul the healthy, unpolluted pleasures of life. I thoroughly enjoy an afternoon of watching a classic movie or musical with my daughters and their girlfriends. Nobody enjoys a night with friends and family more than I do! We play riotous games, listen to country music or Broadway show tunes and laugh the night away. At those times, my soul is filled to overflowing and I am a happy woman!

I'll never forget the evening when my dear cousin, Dan, and his family treated my daughter, Joy, and I to a spectacular summer concert in an outdoor amphitheater. Our souls were thriving and expanding as we listened to the Mormon Tabernacle Choir sing the greatest songs of American History. Over 600 pure, glorious voices robustly sang, "Climb Every Mountain," "This Land is Your Land," and "God Bless America!" My soul was soaring and so I could hardly contain my soulish glee. But, it was not feeding my *spirit*. They were Mormons and had no ability to speak a word of God into the deepest place of me.

Your main attention and focused study needs to be on your spirit, which is the eternal part of you.

"The strong spirit of a man sustains him in bodily pain or trouble; but a weak and broken spirit who can raise up or bear?"
- Proverbs 18:14 (AMP)

Your spirit should be emphatically in charge of your soul if you want to be a healthy woman emotionally. Your soul should at all times bow and submit to your spirit. Your spirit is the 4-star general and your soul is the lowly private and they should treat one another as such. Your spirit should do the commanding and your soul should do the bowing. However, if you continually feed your soul empty calories from the junk food buffet of your emotional outrage and from the fast-food menu of our culture, then your soul will be in charge and your spirit will be the underling.

The Breakfast of Champions

If your desire is to develop a strong spirit, then you must feed it a healthy and vitamin-charged diet. You must read your Bible every day to strengthen the muscles and increase the endurance of your spirit. We primarily read the Bible, not for information, but for transformation and the miracle power found in the Word is an extraordinary vitamin that establishes health in your spirit every single day of your life.

"My soul weeps because of grief; strengthen me according to Your word."

- Psalm 119:28

One of the greatest earthly gifts that I have ever received came packaged as a curly-haired, outspoken, comedienne from Smackover, Arkansas. Her name is Debby and we met the first night of our freshman year in college. Although we were not roommates that first year, we quickly remedied that and roomed together for the next two years. We were total and complete opposites, not only in appearance and heritage, but also in emotional make-up.

Debby was boisterous and loud; I was reserved and measured. Debby had black curly hair with a mind of its own; I had blonde hair that touched my waist. Debby was the life of every party and I never went to parties. Debby spoke with an Arkansas twang that was like fingernails on the chalkboard of life to my refined, Yankee ears. When people on campus heard that we were roommates, we often had to pick their incredulous jaws up off the Oklahoma cement. We had a friendship that was uncommon and continues to this day.

The time-tested memory that I have of this precious friend is that every morning, her alarm went off at the unbelievable hour of 5:30 a.m.! (Before I met Debby, I did not realize that there was a 5:30 a.m.!!) She would leap out of bed, pick up her Bible off her desk and fish for her thick eyeglasses in the dark early hour of the new day. Because I am not a morning person, Debby would thoughtfully tiptoe out into the well-lit dormitory hallway and spend 30 minutes in the Word of God. She had a thematic system that took her through the Bible in a year.

Debby had developed this vital practice when she was 12 years old and her mother had died in her early 30's of breast cancer. The pastor's wife at Debby's church had discipled her with these words, "If you want to walk in victory and overcome your grief, you will need to read your Bible every day." Although Debby missed her mother dearly and longed for the companionship and wisdom that only a mother can give, she suffered no long term negative emotional effects of the tragic event because Debby had fed her spirit and it had become strong and vibrant.

Debby and I graduated from college and both married pastors. Although I could never imagine someone with her buoyancy and free-spirited opinions surviving long as a pastor's wife, she thrived in the position and everyone found her a sheer delight and breath of fresh air. We stayed in touch over the years, exchanging Christmas letters and birthday phone calls. No one ever took her place in my heart.

On April 30, 2005, our family was in Tulsa, Oklahoma, celebrating our second son, Christopher's graduation from college. We were on the lawn outside the massive auditorium taking pictures of grandmothers, aunts, uncles, cousins and siblings with the much-relieved graduate. My phone rang and it was a mutual friend that Debby and I shared. Normally, I would ignore a call like that at such a family-driven moment, but something in my spirit told me to answer the call.

I excused myself and walked under a grove of trees, "Carol, this is Becky and I have called to tell you that Debby's husband, Steve, was killed this morning."

Steve was on a men's retreat with his church and at the end of the teaching time, the men had gathered to do some much needed work on his country home. Steve was on a tractor, pulling down a tree when it tragically changed direction and fell on him. Steve was immediately and gloriously with the Lord and left Debby a young widow at the age of 50.

These are Debby's words of how the Lord met her through her Bible reading the next morning:

I got up early knowing that I had a long and painful day ahead of me. My house was filling with out of town relatives and we had to make funeral plans for my dear husband. I looked at my chart of where I was to read that day and then opened to I Chronicles, chapters 1-8. As I began to read my Bible, I discovered that the entire reading assignment for the day was dead people's names! It was eight solid chapters of nothing but begats. There was no encouragement, no revelation knowledge and no call to worship.

I began to weep and demanded an answer from the Lord, Whom I had served my entire life, "God, you knew that Steve would be in heaven today without me! You knew that I would open my Bible this morning and turn to I Chronicles 1-8! Where are You, God? Why couldn't I be reading in Psalms or the Book of John?!"

As Debby settled down to hear God's voice respond to her, He gently said, "*That's right. I did know that you would need Me today in an extraordinary way. I knew that you would need to hear My voice and I have you right where I want you in the Bible. I wanted to remind you that people are important to Me and that each person lives a life of value in My sight. Steve was important to Me and so are you."*

When Debby heard those words delivered to her heart from heaven's throne room, she once again picked up her well-worn Bible and began to read the record of names in I Chronicles 1: *"Adam, Seth, Enosh, Kenan, Mahalalel, Jared, Enoch, Methuselah, Lamech, Noah, Shem, Ham and Japeth ..."*

God always feeds our spirits through His Word, but most of us lack the discipline and the desire to spend time with Him in this vital way on a daily basis. I pray that you will always remember the story of Debby and her commitment to the Bible. I know that God will do for you what He did for Debby. He will meet you on the worst day of your life and speak strength, hope and concern into your spirit through the miraculous Word of God!

Your choice to feed your spirit healthy nutrients will keep it strong and robust even when your soul is out of control. Reading your Bible on a regular basis is chief among the habits that you need to establish spiritually in order to be a healthy and vibrant woman emotionally. However, there are other ways that you can feed your spirit as well.

A New Wardrobe

One of the most refreshing daily exercises that you will ever participate in is the choice to spend time in worship. It is of vital importance that you understand that the time spent in sheer worship is going to enable you to withstand the storms of life. Worshipping the Lord every day in the shower, while you are driving, or even when you are going for a walk, will give you the perspective of heaven on your situations. Singing while you are doing the dishes and folding laundry will put a spring in your step and joy in your heart. Are you one of those spiritually anorexic Christians who only sing songs of worship on Sundays? You are missing the best part of life! Trust me…you do not want to miss the delight of cleaning the ashes off your life, ridding yourself of the grief and putting on the garment of praise that Jesus has provided for you. It's the greatest exchange in all of recorded history: you give Him your pain and heartbreak and He gives you a garment of praise!

"To grant those who mourn in Zion, giving them a garland instead of ashes, the oil of gladness instead of mourning, the mantle of praise instead of a spirit of fainting. So they will be called oaks of righteousness, the planting of the LORD, that He may be glorified."
- Isaiah 61:3

All women love the story of Esther in the Bible and long for a "happily ever after" story similar to the one that Esther had the privilege of living. The story of Esther has changed my life deeply and has given to me a life strategy of how to conduct my life during difficult days.

Esther was an orphan who had been raised by her bachelor uncle, Mordecai. When King Ahasuerus decided that he wanted a new wife because Queen Vashti had not worked out, his overseers staged the largest beauty pageant in all of recorded history. They brought to the palace all of the beautiful young virgins in the entire kingdom of Persia to compete for the title of Queen for a Lifetime. Believe me when I say that it was no honor to be accepted into this pageant because most of these young women would never again see their families. They might spend one night with the king, but then forever live a life of rejection in the girls' dormitory down some long, lonely hallway of the palace. Their entire life would be like a scene from *The Bachelor*, played out with no ending in sight! Theirs would be a life of catfights, hormonal women and face-scratching to the greatest degree!

Esther won the beauty contest and found favor with everyone inside the palace walls. She was obviously lovely inside and out and King Ahasuerus found her irresistable! Uncle Mordecai daily paced back and forth in front of the gate of the palace, desperately trying to hear a word concerning his beautiful, young niece.

Even in "happily ever after stories," events often take a wretched side road that threaten the lives of the best of characters. Such is the case in the historical account of the newly crowned Queen Esther, King Ahasuerus and Uncle Mordecai.

When Uncle Mordecai refused to bow to Haman, one of the king's chief advisors, it was decided that not only would Mordecai be killed, but Haman received permission from the king that the entire Jewish nation would be slaughtered. When Mordecai learned of this dastardly plan, he tore his clothes, put on sackcloth and ashes and went out into the midst of the city and wailed loudly and bitterly.

Mordecai's response to circumstances that were spiraling out of control, unfortunately, may echo your response to your life's events. When you don't get your way or are faced with impending doom, you follow the example of Mordecai, put on your mourning clothes and then whine and complain so loudly and passionately that the entire city hears you! You might feel that telling your side of the story and making sure that the total universe feels your pain has no eternal consequences, but you are completely wrong. You are utterly and sadly misinformed.

"He (Mordecai) went as far as the king's gate, for no one was to enter the king's gate clothed in sackcloth."

- Esther 4:2

Did you read that? Maybe you need to read it again: "...*for no one was to enter the king's gate clothed in sackcloth.*" This verse is a compelling warning to those of us who love to lament and carry on when life throws a curve ball our direction. If you selfishly and childishly choose to walk through life while dressed in sackcloth and ashes, you will deny yourself intimacy with the King of all kings! Oh...you are still a Christian and you will still spend eternity with Jesus, however, your preoccupation with your pain will deny you the sweetness of cherished fellowship with Him while on planet earth. Your very human need to mourn and lament will not unlock the door that leads to His dear presence.

We mistakenly believe that if we cry out in pain loud enough, we will demand an audience with God. On the contrary, the true password to His presence is thanksgiving!

"Enter His gates with thanksgiving and His courts with praise. Give thanks to Him, bless His name."

- Psalm 100:4

When Queen Esther heard of the pity party that Uncle Mordecai was throwing in front of the king's gates, she sent new garments to Mordecai so that he would remove his sackcloth, but he refused to put them on. The Holy Spirit has given to us a new wardrobe to wear as well, but often we refuse to embrace the garment of praise and instead choose to parade through life in the garment of pain. When you reject the garment of praise and remain inappropriately dressed in the ashes of your past, you are shooting yourself in that infamous foot! The King wants you in His presence! The King of all kings knows that His presence is the place of victorious living for you and the door is thrown wide open for you to enter. Unfortunately, you are unable to walk into the inner courts of His palace while dressed in the disappointment of your circumstances.

The answer to this dilemma is obvious and simple: put on the garment of praise! Rather than writhe in emotional pain…put your hands in the air and sing yourself into His presence!

Prayer Changes Everything

Another way to make sure that your spirit is growing into the most robust part of your inner man is to take the advice of Paul in I Thessalonians 5:17 and pray without ceasing. I did not say whine without ceasing…I said *pray* without ceasing. So many Christian women spend their whole lives whining and complaining to the Lord and then they wonder why their prayers are never answered! When you pray, pray with joy! When you pray, come into His presence boldly and with power! When you pray, leave your emotional soul at the door and take your well-fed spirit into the Throne Room and bask in His wonderful presence!

"Guard your steps as you go to the house of God and draw near to listen rather than to offer the sacrifice of fools; for they do not know they are doing evil. Do not be hasty in word or impulsive in thought to bring up a matter in the presence of God. For God is in heaven and you are on the earth; therefore let your words be few."
- Ecclesiastes 5:1-2

Circle of Friends

The fourth crucial supplement that is required for building a strong spirit is being committed to church and to fellowship with other believers. Do not ever develop the bad habit of being out of the habit of going to church! The Spirit of God truly is present when His

Body gathers together, and He will strengthen your spirit as you discover the joy of corporate worship. God loves His Body of Believers and it is a delight to the heart of our Daddy when we all assemble at the home place for a day of worship, studying the Word of God and fellowship. Not only does He love it…but He loves it when we love it! The concept of church life and gathering together in His Name was His idea from the day that Jesus went back to heaven. The Holy Spirit knew that we would not be able to survive as solo Christians, but we would need the overcoming resources that are presented to us when we huddle together in faith.

"Now My eyes will be open and My ears attentive to the prayer offered in this place. For now I have chosen and consecrated this house that My name may be there forever, and My eyes and My heart will be there perpetually."

- II Chronicles 7:15-16

A Fit and Strapping Spirit

There are other valuable and consistent disciplines that are necessary to adopt in order not only to maintain a healthy spirit, but to assure that it is growing in power and in stamina. I believe that every believer should be committed to a weekly Bible study where the Word is taught in principle and as the absolute Truth. If your desire is to have a fit and strapping spirit, then you also need to be a faithful tither and giver to the Body of Christ.

Feeding your spirit is one of the most paramount determining factors in whether you will be a woman whose emotions are under control or out of control. Either your well-fed soul will control your weak spirit or your healthy spirit will control your soul.

A Soul
Out-of-Control

I love reading the Bible in all of its glorious detail. I especially love the stories of people in the Bible because it reminds me that I don't have to be perfect to serve God and to be used by Him. There is only one perfect Man mentioned in the Bible and His name was Jesus. The rest of the infamous characters in the Word had issues just like you and I do. In some mysterious way, that is a solid and gratifying comfort to my noisy soul. I am greatly relieved when I realize that God used Moses in spite of his low self-esteem and He also used David in spite of his bent toward depression. Saul found twisted pleasure in murdering Christians but the Holy Spirit saw potential in him, renamed him Paul and then wrote nearly half of the New Testament through him! There's hope for me!

There is a man by the name of Peter who is one of the main characters in the New Testament. He was a rugged fisherman with dirt under his fingernails and a loud opinion for every situation. This particular disciple of Christ allowed his emotions to spew out of his mouth in a relentless regurgitation. In all theological descriptions of this eventually powerful man, you will find one common word: impulsive.

Let's eavesdrop on a conversation between the Jesus and the strong-willed Peter that we can find in Matthew 16. I believe that by dissecting this exchange between these two friends, you will learn a lot about yourself. The conversation took place one day when Jesus was walking with His disciples through a particular region known as Caesarea Philippi, which was located several miles north of the Sea of Galilee. This particular territory was highly influenced by the Greek and Roman culture and so pagan temples and idols were found on every street corner. There was hardly a place you could look without being reminded of the hundreds and hundreds of gods who were worshipped by this culture. I can imagine that often as they walked together, Jesus would ask pertinent questions and so this day, as they were surrounded by gods, goddesses and their heathen temples, Jesus posed an interesting question to His band of brothers, *"Who do people say that the Son of Man is?"* (v. 13).

The young men responded eagerly and passionately to their teacher's inquiry, "Well, we have heard some people say that they think you are John the Baptist come back from the dead. Other people wonder if you are Elijah or Jeremiah. Some folks just suppose that you are a prophet. That's what we have heard, anyway." (V. 14.)

Jesus, who is always known for going to the heart of our issues, looked at His dear followers intently, paused for a minute and then quietly asked, *"But who do you say that I am?"* (v.15).

Simon Peter, the bold one who loved Jesus passionately and had left everything to follow Him, responded without a moment's hesitation, "Jesus, you are the Christ! You are the Son of the living God!" (V.16.)

Jesus then smiled, as only Jesus could, and threw His arm around the rugged fisherman's shoulder, "Blessed are you, Simon son of Jonah, because flesh and blood did not reveal this to you, but My Father who is in heaven. Peter…listen to me! You are Peter and you are My rock! I am going to build My church upon this incredible knowledge of exactly Who I am! The gates of Hell itself will have no power to overcome My church!" (Vv. 17-18.)

I bet that Peter couldn't keep his grin to himself and high-fived Jesus with a touch of confidence. Maybe he thought, *Is God really going to use me? All I have done so far is hang around and watch Him do miracles. Is it possible that my life could make a difference in this Kingdom?*

Jesus then offered an intangible, priceless gift to Peter and to all of the Church for the generations to come, *"I will give you the keys of the kingdom of heaven; and whatever you bind on earth shall have been bound in heaven, and whatever you loose on earth shall have been loosed in heaven"* (v. 19).

Scripture was never meant to be read only historically as you would an account of the Civil War or the signing of the Declaration of Independence. The Holy Spirit desires for believers to apply every verse of Scripture to their lives in a personal way. Every story, every piece of theology, every Biblical prayer and verse of praise is able to be applied in a practical sense to your life.

As I read and meditate on this amazing conversation between Jesus and my favorite disciple (sorry John!), I can immediately identify that it was Peter's spirit responding to the Spirit of God. When your spirit talks, it sounds very similar to the Word of God. Your spirit might say, "It's more blessed to give than to receive;" but your soul would assert, "All the church ever talks about is money. Money…money…money."

When going through a particularly difficult time in life, your spirit will remind you, "I can do all things through Christ who gives me strength!" However, your whiney soul will pout and moan, "Why do these things happen to me? Don't I ever get any breaks? Is God out to get me?"

Your spirit, when it is well fed and operating at its optimum level, can respond to gossip and betrayal with a humble, yet positive response, "Lord, I forgive these people right now in Jesus' Name. Please show me how I can bless them and reach out in love." Your soul is always outraged at the difficulty of trying to get along with others and lets the world know, "They can't treat me this way any longer! I am going to give them a piece of my mind!"

When your spirit talks, you will find yourself walking toward your destiny. Jesus embraced the spirit of Peter and told him that He had great plans for Him. When your tongue speaks forth the Word of God and principles of Christ in any situation, you will discover the purposes and plans that the Holy Spirit has for you! When you are walking in the power of your spirit, and not in the excess of your soul, you are given authority in heaven and on earth. The walk of the spirit is always a walk of authority. The walk of the soul is weak, hindered and crippled unless it is coming under the authority of the spirit

Who Will Win?

Peter and Jesus had just had a spirit-to-Spirit bonding conversation, which included a prophetic moment concerning Peter's destiny. Beyond speaking into Peter's life concerning all that was ahead for him, Jesus also had to warn Peter and the others about the difficult days that they were about to face. Jesus wanted to make sure that they were prepared to walk with Him through the last week of His life and all of the persecution that it would entail.

And so, shortly after the scenario that we just witnessed in Matthew 16:13-19, Jesus began to gently share with His disciples that this time of teaching, miracles and evangelism was not going to last forever. Jesus told His team that He would suffer in Jerusalem under the desperate measures of the religious leaders and that He would actually be killed by them, but after three days, He would rise again!

When Peter heard of the gripping future events with which Jesus was attempting to help them cope, he was so overcome with premature grief that he was unable to hear the victorious final part of what Jesus had to say. Peter's soul began to spill out and he began to rebuke Jesus, *"God forbid it, Lord! This shall never happen to You!"* (Matthew 16:22).

Peter's soul was rebuking the Spirit of God and he was reacting to circumstances that he thought were too horrible to face. Peter wanted Jesus to do something to stop these events from unfolding and was unable to hold back his fear and worry.

When we allow our souls to speak out of fear or worry, we are in danger of rebuking the plans and heart of God. We have all been guilty of Peter's sin and have "taken the Lord aside" (Matthew 16:22) to give Him a piece of our mind!

"God! If You loved me, I wouldn't have to go through this!"

"God...I sure hope that You know what You are doing, because I am not getting it!"

"God, I thought that You were in control of my life and yet You allow this to happen?!"

When Jesus turned to look Peter in the eye, He said something so shocking and yet so necessarily bold for Peter's personality and temperament. Those of us who are strong willed and highly influenced by fear and worry have to understand that when you come to the Lord in soulish confusion, you have been influenced by the enemy himself.

"But He (Jesus) turned and said to Peter, 'Get behind Me, Satan! You are a stumbling block to Me; for you are not setting your mind on God's interests, but man's.'"

- Matthew 16:23

Often I have read this very verse and thought to myself, *Oh my! Maybe Jesus wasn't having a very good day! Wow! Peter had really gotten on His last holy nerve!* And then the Holy Spirit reminds me of the intrinsic and eternal truth in this sobering verse: Satan can mess with our emotions and our souls, but never with our spirits. These are among the very strongest of words that Jesus ever spoke to one of His own. Jesus had invested three entire years of 24 hours a day and 7 days a week with Peter and, quite frankly, Jesus thought that Peter should know better by now!

I wonder if Jesus ever thinks that about me…*that I should know better by now!?* When your spirit has been taught by Him and you have read the Word of God and have spent hours in His very presence, Jesus wants to yank your chain away from outrageous emotional and soulish responses to life.

If you read this story of Peter and Jesus without understanding the difference between the soul and the spirit, you would certainly wonder if Peter was schizophrenic or had a split personality. No! We are observing a period in the life of a man who is trying to get his soul to submit to his spirit. I am sure that the Holy Spirit sees me as not much different than Peter. I have moments of great revelation and speak words of power when I allow my spirit to be in authority in my life. But when I panic and push my soul front and center, I am allowing the enemy to influence my ability to cope and to inhibit my ability to walk in victory.

When Peter's spirit was talking, Jesus called him a "rock" and declared over his life that Peter was going to be a significant force in establishing the Church of Christ. When you are feeding your spirit and allowing your tongue to agree with the Word of God, you, too, are a rock in the Kingdom of God. When your responses to life are birthed out of a strong and vital spirit, God can't wait to reveal His plans and purposes to you! God loves using men and women of God who have their souls under submission to their spirits.

However, when Peter's soul forced itself into the driver's seat and when his mouth began to vomit a barrage of emotionally-charged reprimands, he became a stumbling block. Although a stumbling block and a rock may look like nearly the same thing, they are used for two different purposes altogether. A rock is used in the laying of foundations for significant and beautiful buildings; a stumbling block always causes injury and harm.

Your Way or God's Way

What is your heart's desire? Is it to be a rock or a stumbling block? Is it to aggressively share every thought, feeling and opinion that enters your heart and mind? Or is it to control your soul with a spirit that is filled to overflowing with the promises and strength of God? You cannot blame your emotional sludge on your marriage, your parentage or your socio-economic level. Your street address does not determine your emotional health, neither does your income, your health or your friendships. You are the only one who is able to determine whether your spirit will partner with God and be used as a mighty part of His Kingdom at this time in history or if you will allow your soul to express itself with brazen and inappropriate remarks.

"Then Jesus said to His disciples, 'If anyone wishes to come after Me, he must deny himself, and take up his cross and follow Me.'"

- Matthew 16:24

If the desire of your heart is to come after Christ and to pursue Him only, it takes one significant choice. If you want your life to count for something meaningful and to make a difference at this time in history, then your heart's desire will be to press into Christ and to follow Him wholeheartedly. Jesus said in this verse in the Book of Matthew, that the first thing we must do when we choose to join with Christ on our life's journey is to *deny self.*

The world will tell you to exalt yourself and promote self and applaud self. But the way of the world has never been the way of the Word. The Word of God clearly instructs believers from every generation in all of Christendom that in order to follow Christ, you must deny self. Our culture declares that women should express themselves and assert themselves and display themselves. Jesus said, *"Deny yourself."* Who are you listening to on your life's journey? The world? Or the Word? Your culture? Or your Christ?

In this very familiar phrase in Scripture, Jesus is talking to Peter and the disciples, yet His words were meant for us today, as well. Jesus is presenting a life strategy that will enable you to live your best life possible. Jesus, perhaps, is instructing all of us with this insight: *"Don't build a life around what you want! Build your life around Me! If you really desire to live a life that is abundant, then you must deny your soul and feed your spirit."*

Let's now make it practical: What does denying self or denying soul actually mean? What does it mean to feed your spirit?

Your soul may be planning a trip to Hawaii for your fortieth birthday but God's Spirit may speak to your spirit and suggest, *"How about going on a short-term missions trip with your church instead?"*

Your soul, if it is out-of-control, may, like Peter, respond to God with soulish indignation, "But God!! You only turn the big 4-0 one time in your entire life and I have never been to Hawaii! I so deserve this! Besides, You know I hate eating bugs and I absolutely need room service for breakfast."

"Well, if you really don't want to go on a missions trip, how about taking that money and giving it to the youth group at church who is raising funds for summer missions?" God may gently reply.

There will be numerous times when God blesses your heart's desires and you may get to visit Hawaii. (I hope you get to go to Hawaii…I hope that I do, too!) But God will only bless that when your soul is submitting to your spirit. God takes delight in showering us with abundant and lavish blessing when He hears His daughters saying, "Dad, I want Your way! I don't want my way!"

"For whoever wishes to save his life will lose it; but whoever loses his life for My sake will find it. For what will it profit a man if he gains the whole world and forfeits his soul? Or what will a man give in exchange for his soul?"
- Matthew 16:25-26

Now that you know the difference between your soul and your spirit, this verse is going to take on an entirely new and exciting meaning for you. The word that is used for "life" in the passage above is the same word that is used in New Testament Greek to express "soul." If you want to live a life of promise and destiny, then you will lose your soulish responses to life in a relationship with Jesus Christ. You will realize that the proposition that Jesus is offering to you is an opportunity to live with the benefits that only He can offer. Today is your day to lay down your selfish dreams and imaginations and then to retrieve the life that God is offering to you. Today is your day to realize that although you may have accepted Christ as your Lord and Savior decades ago, you have not been living the abundant life that is found only in dying to self and soul. Emotions and passions that seemed so important to express last week or even yesterday now seem futile and fruitless.

Every morning when I wake up, I repeat these words to my sleepy self in the bathroom mirror while brushing my teeth, "I don't get my own way...I don't want my own way...I want God's way!"

For some of you, saying this once a day will be sufficient because your soul and your spirit are already matched in a glorious harmony with the Spirit of the Lord. However, for those of you like me, who have lived a life of stench and worm-infested self, you may have to repeat it every hour...or every minute! But don't worry – your self will eventually "get it," that its free ride is now over and it is time to submit to the spirit that is well-fed and flourishing!

The Bottom Line of Your Soul

"For the Son of Man is going to come in the glory of His Father with His angels, and will then repay every man according to his deeds."
- Matthew 16:27

This is an interesting sequential scripture, after being told the necessity of dying to self. However, if you read it through a couple of times and allow the meaning to sink into your spirit, it is easy to understand the valuable point that Jesus was making to His crew of motley young men.

Your deeds are a reflection of how well you have died to self, soul and passions. It is easy to discern what is going on in a person's soul by observing their deeds. The health and strength of a person's spirit is revealed through the words that they speak, the attitudes that they embrace and the deeds that they do. If one's actions and life choices revolve around self-pleasure and self-absorption, then it is obvious that the soul is in control. However, if one's life is centered around pleasing God and serving others, then it is a surety that a well-nourished and muscular spirit is in charge.

If you want to know the bottom line when it comes to your emotions and estrogen-induced issues, you can absolutely have it your way and feed your soul empty calories, which means that you may gain the world but will definitely forfeit your own soul. The choice is yours and yours alone.

May I give you one last word of advice concerning your soul and your spirit? This is my heartfelt charge and yet practical encouragement for women of every age and in every season of life:

Die to soul...Delight yourself in the Lord...Be fulfilled today and rewarded in the future.

Soulish Prayer

There are four distinct areas of life where the dominance of your spirit agreeing with the Spirit of God is going to yield a vast harvest of fruit. Conversely, if your soul is still calling the shots, it will be in these four areas that you will suffer defeat after defeat.

One of the areas where the control of your spirit is of immeasurable importance is in the area of prayer. When you pray, it should be spirit to Spirit contact; it is a beautiful blending and harmonious response of your spirit reaching out to the Spirit of God. When your spirit talks to the Spirit of God, it is a power talk and a potentially world-changing conversation. When your soul pleads, whines and gripes, it is a conversation of no lasting importance. Your soul always prays from the perspective of self while your spirit prays from the perspective of the Word of God.

Let's listen in on a conversation that a desperate mother is having with the Lord in prayer. This mother is dealing with a child who is choosing to go a rebellious route in life and it is the most difficult experience that this mother has ever had to encounter. However, this mom has only fed her soul empty calories and has paid little or no attention to her spirit. And so, at the most devastating moment in her life, this is the best prayer that she is able to wretch out:

"God, you know I have done my best trying to raise this child. I don't know where I   went wrong. We never had enough money to really give him a great life, and even the kids at church made fun of him. I am at the end of my rope, Lord. I feel like such a failure. God, can't You do anything about my boy?"

This powerless prayer is filled with references to self because our souls always want to be pitied and even to force God into recognizing the martyr status of our soul. A prayer prayed from the never-been-controlled soul selfishly wants God to respond, "Why, of course you have done your best, you poor, pitiful mother! No one appreciates you…no one at church…not your children and not your husband. You deserve so much better than the rotten life you are living!"

Your soul will always endeavor to turn your prayer life into a pity party and so, rather than tapping into heaven's power when you pray, your soul will keep you far away from the dynamic storehouse of God's provision.

On the other hand, a mother who has a strong and well-fed spirit will pray for a wandering child in an entirely different manner. She will be on her knees on a patch of well-worn carpet upon which are imprints from hours spent in this very place. This mother has lived a life of dying to self and cultivating the personality of Christ in her life. She has invested her time in reading the Word, in worship and in service to others. What does a prayer sound like coming from a desperate mother such as this?

"God! You are in control! You are a God of wisdom and might! Your Word says that it is not Your will that one of Your children should perish. You have plans of welfare for my son, to give him a future and a hope. Thank You, Father, for bringing my son back to You!"

This prayer is a beloved litany of the truth found in God's Word and as such, it turns the attention of the prayer warrior toward the heart and throne room of God himself. This prayer is not focused on the very real disappointment of the mother but on the power of the God of all eternity! This prayer turns our hearts and our attentions to the certainty of what God is able to do.

The Desires of Your Heart

The second realm in which you must be influenced by your spirit rather than by your soul is in the scope of your desires.

"The heart is more deceitful than all else and is desperately sick; who can understand it?"
- Jeremiah 17:9

Your heart is extremely loquacious and is certain to tell you everything that it desires. Your heart makes grocery lists, wish lists, Christmas lists and lists of demands. Your heart not only tells you what it wants, but it is also very quick to tell you how it feels about every circumstance in your life. We must always remember that our heart does not tell us the truth. Our heart is not George Washington but is famously known for dealing in deceit and is in the habitual practice of misleading the owner of the heart! If you listen only to your heart, you will end up a victim of emotional chicanery.

Very few women marry the boy that they absolutely could not live without in the eleventh grade. Remember that boy? He was, of course, a football jock and you had his picture up in your locker. You wrote "Mr. and Mrs. Football Jock" on every note from every class and had his phone number written in lipstick on your bathroom mirror. He was all you wanted and you could not imagine a life without him and his All-American good looks! You couldn't eat unless you saw him and every day you memorized what he wore and what he said. At your twentieth class reunion, he had a beer belly, was bald and filled the room with coarse talk and out-spoken opinions. Aren't you thankful that you didn't get what your heart told you that it wanted?!

Your feelings are slippery and they do not bring stability to your life, so be very careful what is crafting your desires. Is it your spirit or your soul?

"Delight yourself in the LORD; and He will give you the desires of your heart."

- Psalm 37:4

Many Christians have mistakenly interpreted this verse to mean that if we dance and sing and raise our hands in God's presence, that we will magically obtain yachts, diamond rings and mansions. The rich and lovely meaning behind these words penned thousands of years ago, yet still true today, is this: when you find your gladness and fulfillment in a relationship with the Lord, He will actually place desires in your heart that are pleasing to Him. He will be the Author of your heart's desires and deepest yearnings and subsequently, He will be the fulfiller of those same desires.

Your soul will perpetually try to derail your life with inappropriate desires and longings, but your spirit will always agree with the Lord and His Word in exactly what is best for you.

Memory

Emotions are a result of the soul's perception of the circumstances in one's life. If you perceive your circumstances filled with doubt, disappointment and bitterness, then the ensuing emotions will never reflect the character and nature of God in your life. However, if you allow your spirit to respond to your circumstances, the emotions that follow may not be emotions at all but may produce the promised harvest of the fruit of the Spirit.

Your soul is also made of the events that have happened in your life and how well or how poorly you responded to those events. Who we are today is the sum of what we have encountered in life and our reactions to those events. Abuses and rejections have hammered women into bruised midgets of who God intended for them to become in Him. Women who have embraced the princess persona are bloated caricatures of the true value that has been placed upon them by the King of all kings.

Our human reactions to all of our life events, whether the event was positive or negative, are poured into our souls and then blended together. What you have named "memory" is, in reality, either your spirit or your soul looking at the history and makeup of your life. The events that you remember with the most clarity and in vivid recall are the ones that have shaped you in greatest detail.

The memories of women who have allowed their emotions to rage inappropriately are a result of their souls' perception of the past circumstances in life. Your soul, when fed with empty calories of junk food living, will sift through past experiences and events and often recall warped remembrances of what actually took place.

Women whose spirits have known the delight of flourishing in God's presence and living according to His principles will respond to their past circumstances, however painful or bitter, with peace and joy.

A soul that has been distended with only vicious and ugly emotions may view its past with these sad words, "I've had a terrible life. You just don't understand my pain. No one has lived through the agony that has impacted my life."

However, a spirit that has known the strength and focus of a life lived wholeheartedly for Christ will look at the past with this wisdom and peace, "I have not encountered one obstacle that God has not used for His purposes. In every challenge and through every heartache, He has been with me."

It is imperative that you look back at your life through the power of your spirit and not through the instability of your soul. Your soul will make absolutely sure that you regret certain events and carry life-long bitterness toward people who mistreated you. If you have lived a wonderful life, your soul will contaminate even the joy of those memories. Your soul tied you to your past with an unhealthy, emotional cord and so will continually cause you to long for the "good-old days" to such an extent that you will not be living in the present. Your soul has been shaped by how well or how poorly you have handled past experiences in life.

Your spirit will look back at your life experiences, both painful and lovely, and will be filled with gratefulness at God's faithfulness. Your spirit will continuously point out the fingerprint of God in all of your life's situations.

"Brethren, I do not regard myself as having laid hold of it yet, but one thing I do: forgetting what lies behind and reaching forward to what lies ahead, I press on toward the goal for the prize of the upward call of God in Christ Jesus."

- Philippians 3:13-14

We cannot alter our past, but we can place our past on the altar as an act of worship and sacrifice to the Lord. A worshipping heart will allow God to restore your soul and meet you in those very difficult moments of life. We all have experienced both the good and bad of life, as well as disappointments and incredible victories. However, for life to be good at its very core, we must allow God to reach into our experience and then redeem us from all negative reactions.

One Defining
Moment

What is your favorite word? I asked a group of world-changing women of God what their favorite words were and here is the list that they came up with:

Forgiveness
Christmas
Family
Mother
Celebrate
Emma

I am sure that you can guess that the last word in the list came from the heart of a young mother who is absolutely enamored with her little bit of feminine potential in the form of her newborn baby! I like all of those words and understand why women would love each one of them. My favorite word, however, was birthed in my heart when I was just a little girl helping my dad in the family garden.

My dad was a farmer at heart and loved every minute of the long summer afternoons when he spent time in the plot of land behind our country home. Because I was always a daddy's girl, when he was out digging in the dirt, so was I! When he was weeding and whistling, I was his partner. And when it came time to harvest the yearly abundance, I loved the evenings of canning and freezing together in our pink and green kitchen.

I will always remember the lesson that my wise father taught me early one Saturday morning on the plot of land that nurtured our garden. My sister and I had fought the night before and it had escalated out of control. Both of us had said things that were unkind and uncalled for and because my father was a godly man who loved peace in his home, we not only hurt one another with our verbal battle but we had wounded our father and all that he stood for.

Dad and I were almost to the harvest stage of the annual garden and so we were beginning to observe that which would be harvested in only a matter of days. We came upon a section in the garden that was close to our neighbor's yard which their dog had claimed as his very own. He had plopped himself upon it one too many times and then he had expressed his bodily functions day after day on this particular one foot by two foot slice of our garden, which was now absolutely ruined. The plants were flattened and brown with no hope of a harvest. The vines had separated from the stem of the plant and the nearly indiscernible breeze that day caused each dead leaf to break away from the root system.

Right next to the mutilated section of the garden was one of the most fruitful portions of our family garden. It received just the right amount of sunlight and rain; we had weeded it to perfection and every leaf was green and vibrant. The harvest was going to be delicious and abundant.

"Carol," my dad quietly said, "why is that one section of our garden so dry and brown and dead?"

"Well," I replied in my best 10-year-old voice, "it is because that horrible dog from next door did his business all over our garden."

"That's right," Dad patiently replied. "Now, take a look at this section of our garden and tell me why it is so beautiful."

Although this question was a bit more complicated for my young philosopher's brain, I was able to respond, "I think that it is because we treated it right. We watered it and weeded it and fertilized it, and so it grew."

My dad squatted beside me in the damp, early morning dirt and paused, "Carol, life is like that. If you treat something unkindly it will die. But if you treat it with love and care, it will flourish."

Although I was only one decade old, I still understood the lesson that Daddy was trying to teach me. My heart stopped and I threw my arms around his neck. "I am so sorry, Daddy. I will never talk like that again. Please forgive me."

Forgiveness was quickly given and I wiped my tears away with the dirt of the garden smudging my cheeks. The word that I carried from that heartfelt experience was the word "flourish" and it has been a treasure in my heart every decade since.

Me and God!

"The righteous man will flourish like the palm tree, he will grow like a cedar in Lebanon. Planted in the house of the LORD, they will flourish in the courts of our God. They will still yield fruit in old age; they shall be full of sap and very green, to declare that the LORD is upright; He is my rock, and there is no unrighteousness in Him."

- Psalm 92:12–15

God made you to flourish and to inexhaustibly thrive. He did not make you to die on the vine of life. He spiritually designed you for emotional and spiritual abundance in every season of your life. His plan was never that you would be shriveled up emotionally and trampled upon by anger and depression and worry. God's intent was that you would not live a brittle life, but would live a life that flourishes. God knew that we would all experience vicious windstorms and the pollution of our culture, but His creative genius provided a way to stay connected to the Vine during all of life's erratic seasonal changes. God's will for you is to flourish in every area of your life and that includes in your emotions!

The word "flourish" is a Hebrew word that is rich in meaning and in usage. It always refers to something or someone who is growing by those infamous leaps and bounds. "Flourish" is a word picture of a plant that is destined to grow abundantly regardless of the climate or drought. As I study this word that was introduced to me while still a child, I realize that flourishing emotionally requires two primary influencers: me and God.

The Psalmist declares that, *"the righteous man will flourish like the palm tree."* If the Bible uses the word "righteous" to describe a person, it means that this person has willfully chosen to connect himself or herself to God. It does not mean that the described person is perfect, but it does mean that the person has chosen to put on God's imputed righteousness. You will flourish, then, in direct proportion to your connection with God! If you choose to bask in His presence on a daily basis and spend time in the Word and in prayer, your life will be a grand display of the growth that comes from your connection to His righteousness. If you choose only to water your life with His sustaining presence on Sunday mornings, then your life will look much like that little plot of ground that my neighbor's dog sat upon.

To whom or to what are you connected? Many Christians are more connected to the pain of their past than they are to the reality of God's presence on a daily basis. It really does matter to you emotionally whether or not you read your Bible every day. It really does matter to you emotionally whether or not you worship in spite of your disappointment. It really does matter to you emotionally if you pray for those who have been unkind to you. It really does matter.

The second influencer, and the most vital one, in your ability to flourish is God! When you choose well, God will cause the growth! You will begin to grow by leaps and bounds both spiritually and emotionally because you are receiving life from God. The fruit of the Spirit will miraculously make you into someone who has the temperament and personality of God. You will look at yourself and declare incredulously, "Self…who are you and what did you do with your sorry old self?!" Well, the answer to that tongue-in-cheek question is this: I am flourishing and becoming who God wanted me to be before the beginning of time. My sorry old self is no more and has been buried along with anger, bitterness, worry and whining.

When you choose to be in vital connection with Jesus on a daily basis, the life that you will receive from Him will grow you into the person that God had in mind the day that He created you. You must work in tandem with God in the garden of your heart until your emotional responses to the climate around you are the result of your deep and rich connection with Him. He gives to you what you could never instigate in your own strength. You can't do it without Him, and He won't do it without you!

Chicken Doo-Doo, George Washington and Green Paint

When my mom and dad were newlyweds in the 1950's, they were given an old, beat-up dresser from my father's parents. This dresser had been in their chicken shed for many decades, but my well-meaning paternal grandmother thought that my parents could put it to good use in their eclectic, newlywed home. This dresser was covered with years of dust, chicken doo-doo and countless feathers from generations of hens. My grandmother tried cleaning it up but found it impossible, so she just covered all of that residue with a coat of ugly, olive green paint.

This dresser sat in our upstairs hallway for all of my childhood. We used it for storing dress-up clothes and tinker toys. In the top drawer, there were piles of construction paper, Crayola crayons and permanent markers. It stayed that putrid shade of olive green until I left for college in the summer of 1973.

As I grew up and left my girlhood behind, my mom finally decided to have the pea-green paint removed from that dresser in hopes that she would pass it on to me someday. She took it to a family friend, Mr. Cianfrini, who had established a refinishing business in his garage during his retirement years. Mom often took pieces of furniture to Mr. Cianfrini, who restored scratched and stained pieces of wooden furniture to their original glory.

My mom dropped the dresser off on her way to work one morning, and the very next day, Mr. C. called and told her to come by and pick it up. She couldn't imagine that he had refinished such a damaged piece of furniture so quickly and asked him how he had completed it in a mere 24 hours.

Mr. C. explained, in his thick Italian accent, that as he took a thorough look at this olive green dresser and then researched its features in a book that identified expensive antiques, he realized that this dresser was made during the Revolutionary War and that it was a priceless heirloom. Mr. C. said that it was reminiscent of furniture made for George Washington himself! He refused to touch it and encouraged my mother to take it to a professional craftsman. He said that it was worth tens of thousands of dollars... potentially even more.

Mom insisted that Mr. C. was the one that she wanted to restore this unique piece of history. She trusted him and knew that whatever he touched, he did so with loving care. It took Mr. C. months to painstakingly restore this dresser to its original condition. Gently, oh so gently, he removed the horrid paint...and then the grime...and finally the stains. When Mr. C. had removed all the dirt, he began to buff the dresser...to varnish it...and to restore it to its intended beauty.

You are that dresser...you were made to be valued and cared for. But instead, you have chosen to live in the chicken coop of life and it has camouflaged you with doo-doo, feathers and decades of dirt. If that weren't enough pain, some well-meaning, self-help guru has painted you an unnatural, vomitus hue. God desires to remove all of that and to slowly, gently and lovingly restore you to the natural beauty of His creation. Will you allow Him to do that? Will you remain in His presence long enough for Him to clean you up so that He can show you off? Your life is not your own, you know, but you have been created in His image to be part of His strategy at this time in history.

Your Defining Moment

We all have a defining moment in life that has determined our emotional stability, habits and structure. For some, it has been a trauma-induced event, like a soldier who suffers from post traumatic stress disorder. Every word that you speak is colored by that traumatic event and every decision that you make is undeniably influenced by that moment.

Perhaps it is not trauma that has shaped your emotional responses to life, but quite simply a lifetime of disappointment has caused you to be a critical person. Because of the black haze that surrounds your life, nothing is ever good enough for you nor is anyone ever kind enough. You mark everyone else's life with your red grading pen and with the words, "Wrong! Wrong! Wrong!"

Many women I meet are the victims – and I do mean victims – of the princess persona. These particular women pirouette their way through everyone else's ordinary life and allow the world to watch their self-appointed royal highness twirl as they perform on their self-constructed majestic platform. Women who are trapped inside the princess persona freely speak their minds and pose opinions for their entire universe to see. Because, after all, the world does belong to the princess. These women make sure that they get their way all the time and that everyone else bows as they pass by.

What has created your emotional imbalance? Have you figured it out yet? Is there a reason why you are not flourishing? What have you allowed to cover your life with chicken doo-doo and putrid colors?

For David, it was a child that died too early. For David, it was a little boy who died because of his own sin.

> *David therefore inquired of God for the child; and David fasted and went and lay all night on the ground. The elders of his household stood beside him in order to raise him up from the ground, but he was unwilling and would not eat food with them. Then it happened on the seventh day that the child died. And the servants of David were afraid to tell him that the child was dead, for they said, "Behold, while the child was still alive, we spoke to him and he did not listen to our voice. How then can we tell him that the child is dead, since he might do himself*

harm!" But when David saw that his servants were whispering together, David perceived that the child was dead; so David said to his servants, "Is the child dead?" And they said, "He is dead."

- II Samuel 12:16-19

I cannot imagine a pain more horrific or paralyzing than the pain of losing a child. I know women who have lost children to tragic accidents and to appalling illnesses and, quite frankly, I wonder how they are continuing to breathe. Watching one of your children die must stir up emotions so raw and deep that performing a necessary daily act like eating is torturous and holding a normal conversation is like running the gauntlet. Parents who have buried a child often tell me that looking ahead is devastating: there really is nothing to dream about or plan for.

If anyone deserved to hate himself, it was David. If anyone deserved to crawl into the black, bottomless pit of depression and never come out again, it was David. But, what you deserve to do and what you should do are two different roads entirely.

"So David arose from the ground, washed, anointed himself, and changed his clothes; and he came into the house of the LORD and worshiped. Then he came to his own house, and when he requested, they set food before him and he ate."

- II Samuel 12:20

After the premature death of David's young son, he willfully chose to perform five distinct actions. David arose from the ground, he washed himself, he anointed himself, he changed his clothes and finally, he worshipped. We are going to study each one of those indi-

95

vidual actions because I believe that each action will heal you as you deal with traumatic events that you have experienced.

First of all, David *"arose from the ground."* As I study this phrase in the ancient Hebrew, I find that what David did was he arose out of the dirt which is symbolic of the pain of his circumstances. He established himself away from the horror of the moment and actually moved forward. David decided to leave the pain behind him so that he could move ahead into the plan of God for his life. As Christian women, no matter what trauma we have experienced, we must rise up and move forward away from our pain and away from all of the events that are keeping us from flourishing. Like David, we need to let our past be our history and not our future.

The second decision that David made was to *"wash himself."* You, too, must rid yourself of the dirt, pain and disappointment that tries to cling after traumatic events. I often pray, "Holy Spirit, wash me! Cleanse me from residual dirt that is trying to cling to my soul."

Step one is getting up from the ground, but often there remains a residue of despair after the traumatic event. Washing yourself may include finding a Christian counselor and spending months under their guidance. Washing yourself may also include confession or finding a friend who will faithfully pray for you and with you. Do whatever it takes to rid yourself of the residue of pain.

The third thing that David did was that he *"anointed himself."* In the Old Testament, anointing always took place after the washing or the bathing. Anointing is always symbolic of preparing yourself for God's service and for ministering to others; it always involves a giving of oneself. After dealing with unimaginable pain, David prepared himself to serve God and to give to others. Most of us would rather curl up in a fetal position and never interact with others again. What you feel like doing and what you should do are two different things. What you feel like doing may not be the healthiest or the godliest option that you have. Do not waste your pain, but use it as a springboard for service to others. If you have had an abortion, volunteer at a pregnancy crisis center. If you have a child on drugs, teach Sunday School and love other people's children. If you are a widow, offer to babysit for a young couple who cannot afford a baby sitter.

The fourth thing that David did was he *"changed his clothes."* David removed his garment of mourning and put on a garment of praise. He prepared himself for time in God's presence. When you have walked through an event of tragedy and unthinkable grief, like David, you need to change your clothes.

"To grant those who mourn in Zion, giving them a garland instead of ashes, the oil of gladness instead of mourning, the mantle of praise instead of a spirit of fainting. So they will be called oaks of righteousness, the planting of the LORD, that He may be glorified."

- Isaiah 61:3

The fifth choice that David made while he was still in the throes of grief was that *"he came into the house of the Lord and worshiped."* If you long to flourish and to move beyond the pain and disappointment then this is what you will do: *You will worship!* David chose to move past his emotional pain and into his destiny. While you are gasping for air, you will lift your hands heavenward and emphatically declare the goodness and faithfulness of God. We have been given very powerful weapons to use while reaching for an abundant life, and worship is one of these weapons. Worship is one of the most powerful cleansing agents to deal with the pain of your past. Worship will heal your mind and your memories; it will take the power out of your pain and restore you to emotional health. Worship does not ignore or minimize the pain of your past, but it keeps the pain in your past and not in your present or in your future.

The Big
3

Emotions! Those tornadoes that blow into our lives, cause some damage, and then run away again. Now, granted, some pleasant emotions such as happiness, contentment, delight or gratitude may lovingly decorate our lives like a spring day but others hold the power of a strong and overpowering storm. There are many emotions that stand poised and ready to destroy whomever and whatever is in their destructive pathway.

I believe that there are three emotions that, although they target men as well as women, are particularly lethal in a woman's life. This powerful triumvirate of assaulting emotions has the potential to tear up the beauty of your life and hold you captive for decades. There is not a woman in the world who has not experienced the emotional challenge of weariness, fear and loneliness. When experienced singularly, they are daunting at best but when faced as a powerful corporate stronghold, it is impossible to overcome them without divine intervention. Weariness, fear and loneliness are three emotions that taunt women in the 21st Century and certainly may stunt all potential for healthy growth. The Bible addresses these three emotions and also has answers for those who are found paralyzed in their colossal path.

History Is Good for You

May I give you some Bible history before we place these three emotions under our microscope of Scripture? Many of the chapters in the Old Testament that precede the Book of Psalms are books of warfare which detail battles of good versus evil and right versus wrong. God was infiltrating an extremely barbaric society with His Name and His ways. God was introducing His commandments and His benefits to a sinful and prideful group of early human beings. God's will was never for mankind to kill one another and so He told the people through Moses, *"Thou shall not kill"* (Exodus 20:13 KJV). Why then, is this brutal history of mankind included in the Holy Bible?

As I read these books of Bible history, I am always reminded that I, too, have an enemy whose desire it is to kill me and to destroy my life. My enemy does not fight fair and is barbaric at best. My enemy, also known as Satan or the father of all lies, has one goal and that is to ruin any hope that I have of living an abundant life. He is not able to take eternity away from me so he claws and grabs at my emotional life in a desperate attempt to paralyze my heart.

Eavesdropping

Let's listen in on a private conversation between Ahitophel and Absalom who were plotting and conniving about how to kill King David. Ahitophel was formerly one of David's closest advisors but chose to betray King David and turn his back on the king. Ahitophel, because he knew King David so well, gave advice to Absalom about how he could defeat and then assasinate the king.

"I will come upon him while he is weary and exhausted and terrify him, so that all the people who are with him will flee. Then I will strike down the king alone."

- II Samuel 17:2

Your enemy has a strategy of how to defeat you and it is not much different from that of Ahitophel. Your enemy's goal is for you to be weary and exhausted every day of your life. Your adversary would like nothing better than for you to be terrified and filled with fear. And finally, your enemy wants you alone. All alone.

Weariness, fear, and loneliness are three emotions that taunt women of every age and at every time in history. The good news is this: Jesus is not surprised by these three emotions and His plan trumps that of the enemy every single time! There is power in the Word of God to fight every negative emotion and to dismantle the schemes and plans of his royal nothingness.

Weariness

A Bible dictionary defines weariness as, "exhaustion; to be faint; to wear out or be worn out; tired, sick, fatigued, exhausted and out of patience."

Perhaps the Bible dictionary just described you! In any case, that is the "you" that the enemy wants you to be. Satan is conniving, deceptive and secretive and he will wear you out any way that he is able to do so. The route to weariness is a short one and you will arrive at exhaustion sooner than you dare believe.

Most of the Christian women I know are worn out from over-spending and overeating; they are exhausted from over-committing to the wrong things and under-committing to all the right things. Stress is not merely just a result of trying to attempt to do too much, but it is spending your time doing things that leave you unfulfilled and empty.

Women are always in a hurry, have you noticed? We hurry to potty train our children and then hurry them off to pre-school so we can have more leisure time. And yet, when the kids finally leave home, we long for the days when they would put their little arms around our necks. But we hurried through all that.

We hurry through the grocery store because we have to make it to the drug store, the gym and the dry cleaners before 5:00. And in our hurry to check things off our "to do" list, we miss the elderly man who needs a word of encouragement and never even think to help the young mom with three toddlers and a cart filled with groceries.

We hurry through high school so we can grow up and be an adult who hurries through life and ends up in middle age a tired, weary, uncreative woman who says, "Why was I in such a hurry?"

The devil, who is your arch-enemy, wants you to be worn out and run ragged through your entire life. As you fill your life with stuff, things and busyness, he is laughing hysterically at you knowing that he just won this battle.

"He will speak out against the Most High and wear down the saints of the Highest One...."

-Daniel 7:25

Satan is wearing down the saints of the Most High God with busyness and the tyranny of the urgent. Why are you listening to his strategies? Satan knows that you will lose every battle you face if he can wear you down. What will you lose? Not your eternal salvation, of course, but you will lose your temper and your patience. You will also lose your perspective and your peace of mind. You might lose your creativity and your daily disciplines.

We mistakenly believe that it is more important to sign our children up for soccer than it is to place the Word of God in their hearts. We wrongly think that cutting coupons is just as important as praying for the president, our pastor and our family. God has a perfect plan and will for your life – and so does the devil. The devil's plan is to keep you so busy and distracted from the primary issues of life that you live a run-down, worn-out existence rather than an abundant life.

The devil is an expert in trickery and in distraction. The devil does not tempt you with blatant evil but with things that seem good. Satan will use something that appears momentarily good to call you away from God's best for your life. What good thing is distracting you from God's best today? Good things may wear you down, but God's best will always strengthen you and bring peace to your life.

Perhaps it is time for you to make some much needed changes in your life. You may need to re-order your daily schedule or re-prioritize your time commitments. Ask a friend to help you re-organize your life so you live abundantly and not as a worn-out, run-down shrew.

Often when I am feeling overwhelmed, I declare to the devil and all of his wimpy nincompoops, "You are not going to wear me down...I am going to wear you down with worship and the Word of God!" After you make that declaration, then begin to reevaluate your choices so that you break the cycle of weariness in your life. Choose to spend time with the Lord rather than spending your day talking on the phone or playing computer games. Speak psalms and hymns and spiritual songs over your life rather than spouting opinions and gossip and frustration. Purpose today that you will no longer invest yourself in urgent demands, but that you will devote yourself to eternal, important disciplines. Trust me, you will only need to make a few strategic choices to replace your weariness with God's perfect peace.

"Abide in Me, and I in you. As the branch cannot bear fruit of itself unless it abides in the vine, so neither can you unless you abide in Me."

- John 15:4

God has an anecdote for weariness; He has prescribed "abiding" for your tired and exhausted soul. The spiritual opposite for weariness is the simplicity of abiding in Christ.

We are to remain in constant, unbroken fellowship with Jesus Christ. This is not a once a week visit, but we are invited to build a life around His presence. The welcome mat is out for you to make His presence your true home. His presence is not meant to be a respite from the storm or a lovely vacation home, but it is a place in which you can build your life and never, never leave! When your permanent residence is the presence of Christ and you allow Him to whisper in your ear a plan for each day, every hour and even the specific moments of your day, it is then that His glorious fruit will be beautifully evident and deliciously apparent in your well-watered life.

The word "abide" in the Greek is translated as "to last or endure." When you abide in Christ daily as you continually fill yourself with the manna of His Word and refresh yourself in the cool stream of worship, you will most certainly outlast the devil and his strategies for you. You will no longer be a woman who is stressed out and weary but you will be a picture of health and cultivated loveliness as you simply abide in Christ.

Olympic Worriers

The second strategy of the devil with which he endeavors to defeat you is to fill your heart with fear and worry.

"I will come upon him while he is weary and exhausted and terrify him, so that all the people who are with him will flee. Then I will strike down the king alone."
— *II Samuel 17:2*

I know many Christian women who are champion worriers. They could win an Olympic gold medal in worrying! If these worriers ever find themselves unworried, they begin to worry that there is nothing to be worried about!

Some Christian women are mere recreational worriers and when their minds are not busy with something significant, they revert to worry. This is what the thought processes of a recreational worrier sound like: *Oh, I've got nothing better to do today...I think that I will just set my legs up and worry a spell.*

Some Christian women would rather worry than eat chocolate...now I don't understand a woman like that! I have a friend who worries that she doesn't trust God enough and so she is worried about how much she does or does not worry.

"For God has not given us a spirit of timidity, but of power and love and discipline."
— *II Timothy 1:7*

If you have a problem with fear and worry, I can tell you exactly where it came from! Women who have downloaded fear and worry onto their mental hard drive get their primary information from the devil himself. Ladies, let me be blunt here…you are listening to the wrong voice! You have bought the wrong newspaper! Put that gossip rag where it belongs…in the trashcan! You are accepting gifts from the wrong person! Change the channel! Press the mute button and open the Bible! There is a spiritual mafia and if I were you, I would not get messed up in their plans. If the devil is your primary source of information, you will be in over your head and will have to run for your life!

The devil wants you exhausted and worn out; there is nothing the devil hates more than a woman of God who has learned the secret of abiding. Satan wants you to get your information from him and not from the Word of God. Worry and fear will rip your abundant life right out of your sweaty, little hands.

The Greek word for "fear" in both the Ancient Hebrew and the Greek, implies a fleeing or a running away from something or someone. So, when the Bible instructs us to "fear not" it is in essence saying, "Don't run away!" Very few of us actually run away physically from a situation that frightens us, but where we actually run away is in our minds. We allow our minds to run like that infamous chicken with its head cut off and we imagine all sorts of sordid and ridiculous scenarios.

When a child is 15 minutes late getting home from school, we imagine that someone has kidnapped him or her and that we will never seen them again. *Fear not!*

If you wake up two mornings in a row with a headache, you wonder if it could be a brain tumor. *Fear not!*

You've gained a little weight and your husband forgot your anniversary so you wonder if there could be another woman. *Fear not!*

The words "fear not" appear in tandem at least 144 times in the Bible. And when the Bible says "fear not," it means do not run away. When you are afraid or worried, rather than running away, you need to run forward into all that God has for you. The reason that Satan tries to give you a spirit of fear is so that you will run away from the blessings and power of God. The opposite of running away is pressing forward. When you are a daughter of the Most High God and know the reality of serving Christ, you press forward. Do not linger over another thought that comes from the father of all lies but press on toward the goal!

"Not that I have already obtained it or have already become perfect, but I press on so that I may lay hold of that for which also I was laid hold of by Christ Jesus. Brethren, I do not regard myself as having laid hold of it yet; but one thing I do: forgetting what lies behind and reaching forward to what lies ahead, I press on toward the goal for the prize of the upward call of God in Christ Jesus."
- Philippians 3:12-14

If you are running scared, you are running backwards into your past and away from the arms of God. If you are pressing ahead, you are moving toward the prize of the upward call of God in Christ Jesus! You will only find the presence and power of God as you press ahead, not if you run away scared.

Most of us are not afraid of the big, bad wolf or of the dark or even of sudden and widespread disaster but what truly frightens us is rejection and failure and people. You should never begin a sentence with the words, "I'm afraid...." As women who love and trust God, we never make a decision based on fear but based on faith in a mighty big God who is well able to take care of every detail.

Knowing that you have not been given a spirit of fear from God, what has God given to you? He has given to you a spirit of power and love and a sound mind. Your mind needs to receive the message that you are one powerful chick! Did you know that the devil knows that you are powerful? He just doesn't want you to know that you are powerful! Declare it today…out loud…and unafraid:

I am a woman of power!

I will not run scared but I will press forward into all that God has for me!

There…didn't that feel good?

Friends Don't Let Friends Worry

I refuse to let my friends worry. If anyone in my family or within my circle of friends begins to worry, I begin to quote the Word of God. Now, I am sure that I might come across as obnoxious when I do this but I find it obnoxious that they worry! How dare they have a shadow of doubt that God is not in control? Don't they know that God is good all the time and that He has plans for welfare and not calamity for them? If they accuse me of not understanding, I gently say, "I think that you are the one who doesn't understand. You don't understand the nature and character of God. He has been to your future and it is good!"

If you want to be my friend, we will not worry together, we will not worry alone, but we will be women of God who trust all the time, every time! I use my words as strategic weapons of warfare that display my faith in an all-powerful God. Worry is always a waste of time and of valuable energy. There are prayers to be prayed and people who need to be loved…there are books to be written and kindness that needs to be shown. When you worry, Satan grins. I refuse to make Satan grin, but I am determined to make Satan worry. He better be worried about the women who live today because we are one powerful fighting force and we will stand toe to toe and nose to nose with the accuser of the sistern and declare, *You are going down, butt head!*" (Disclaimer: I only use the words "butt head" together when I am talking about Satan. I promise.)

Fleeing Friends

"I will come upon him while he is weary and exhausted and terrify him, so that all the people who are with him will flee. Then I will strike the down the king alone."

- II Samuel 17:2

A result of being weary, exhausted and afraid is that everyone around you will surely flee. It is nearly impossible for an exhausted, fearful woman to maintain healthy relationships. Flourishing women have absolutely no desire to maintain relationships with worriers because of the drain that it causes in every area of the relationship. It is heartbreakingly difficult to nurture a friendship with someone who is always weary and stressed out because they are always complaining about how much they have to do and how tired they are. Worriers and stressed out women tend to adopt a martyr's complex and thereby cause dear friends and family members to run away from intimacy with them. If you desire healthy, vital relationships, you will abide and not be stressed out! If your heart's desire is a delightful smorgasbord of friendships, then you will trust the Lord wholeheartedly and refuse to ever worry again.

One Is the Loneliest Number

"Then I will strike the king down alone."

- II Samuel 17:2

Loneliness is simply feeling like no one really cares about you or about your life. It is thinking that nobody wants to listen to you or really know what is going on in your heart. It is believing that even if you did have a friend who knew your whole heart, that they wouldn't like it or accept it at all. Loneliness very well may be the most destructive emotion of all. If Satan is not able to trip you up with worry and fear, he will try to alienate you from healthy relationships because even Satan knows the power of two!

"Again I say to you, that if two of you agree on earth about anything that they may ask, it shall be done for them by My Father who is in heaven. For where two or three have gathered in My Name, I am there in their midst."

- Matthew 18:19-20

Although you may *feel* alone, you must remind yourself that you are never really alone because the Bible promises it.

"I will never desert you, nor will I ever forsake you."

- Hebrews 13:5

This is one of those strategic life moments when you must remind yourself that all of your feelings are not valid. When your heart tries to tell you that you are all alone and that no one cares about you or your life, your heart has been communing with Satan and listening to his dastardly lies.

"The heart is more deceitful than all else and is desperately sick; who can understand it?"

- Jeremiah 17:9

When it comes to loneliness, you must open your Bible and agree with the Word of God and not with your pitiful feelings. The last words that Jesus spoke to His disciples reminded them that even though they would not be able to see Him anymore with their eyes, that He really would be with them always: *"I am with you always, even to the end of the age"* (Matthew 28:20).

The theme song of Jesus is that you will never walk alone. Never. The lie that Satan vomits up addresses only our feelings and is not a spiritual reality. The Biblical reality is that you are surrounded by God's love and care every day of your life. There is nothing that can separate you from the love of God; you are securely surrounded by His loving care because He has promised it. Loneliness is a lie...a spiteful and hateful lie that will cause you to question the truth of God's infallible Word.

Jesus really is your best friend, so begin to act like it today. Feel free to talk to Him at anytime...any place...or anywhere. Share your heart with Jesus and then listen to hear how He responds to you. Serve Him everywhere you go and never forget that you will never be able to out give Him, although it is a whole lot of fun to try! Make dates with Jesus and don't just "pencil" Him in but make a date and then keep it! Spend an entire evening in His presence with worship music playing and the Word of God open. Write Him long and intimate love letters and sing out your heart while you are in His presence. I have been known to enjoy a good laugh with Jesus and I must tell you, I love spending time in His arms dancing the night away! When you begin to respond to Jesus as you would to a friend, your loneliness will ebb away – I guarantee it!

Feelings do not deal in the truth but love to throw a pity party and invite you to come as the only guest. While your feelings may tell you that you are all alone, let me remind you that the Bible instructs believers how to access the presence of God.

Access the Presence

"For where two or three are gathered together in my name, there am I in the midst of them."

- Matthew 18:20 (KJV)

This scripture reminds us that when we are with each other, He is with us. If you want to spend time with God, try spending an evening with a group of people who love Him. If you feel alone, invite some people over who love to pray and guess Who else will walk in your door?

"But thou art holy, O thou that inhabitest the praises of Israel."
- Psalm 22:3 (KJV)

God dwells where praise is full and strong. If you want Him to make Himself real and known to you, then you should spend your life worshipping Him. God shows up when a man or woman of God defies events and circumstances with a heart overflowing with pure worship. If you deal with loneliness, turn up the worship music and lift your hands in the air because He is there! You are not alone. Sing out loud and sing out strong! He is there! You are not alone. Sing in the car and in the shower and He will be with you. Whenever you make a conscious choice to worship, you have just placed yourself in His presence. You are not alone. Ever.

Don't Be Passive

If I was a doctor, and I suppose that I am…I am a doctor of the soul, so let me write you a prescription for loneliness. Give to someone else at least three times a day. Your loneliness will be cured when you are more concerned about someone else's needs rather than your solitary life. Smile at someone in the grocery store aisle. Write an old college friend a note and reconnect with her. Do not be passive and stay at home watching television, because you will find that giving is always the cure for loneliness.

When I was a freshman in college, I was morbidly homesick the first semester. I was attending a well-respected Christian university over 1,000 miles away from my safe, loving home. I did not want to return to the university after Christmas break but my father made me return saying that I needed to finish what I had started. One winter evening in January, I was crying in my wing chaplain's room, telling her how lonely I was and how much I hated living away from home. Tanya was quietly writing on a piece of paper while I was sobbing and gulping, which was giving way to near hysteria. When my diatribe calmed down, she quietly handed me the piece of paper, which had a list of assignments on it:

1 – *Do not walk with your head down as you cross campus. Look people in the eye and smile.*

2 – *Leave the door to your room open – don't close it.*

3 – *On Friday evenings, make popcorn in your room and let the smell waft into the hallway.*

4 – *Don't stop at the desk and look to see if there is a note for you. Write someone else a note. Every day.*

5 – *When you go to the cafeteria for dinner, you are not allowed to sit alone. Ever. Find a group of people, ask if you can join them, sit down and introduce yourself. Enter into their conversation.*

Tanya knew that I had developed some horrible habits during my fits of homesickness and her goal was to break me of the unhealthy social choices I had been making. The list was only the beginning of her remedies because as I walked out of her room that night, she handed me her popcorn popper and an entire box of stationery to ensure that I would follow through on her "to-do" list.

The first time that I walked into the cafeteria after having been given my life-altering commandments, I found a table where a young man and young woman were sitting together and shyly asked if I could join them. I recognized them as important upperclassmen and thought, *If I can build a friendship with them, I might be important someday, too!*

The young woman hesitated but finally said "Sure," and the young man just looked away. I could tell right away that I was unwanted but didn't know how to gracefully excuse myself. I quickly wolfed down my dinner in five minutes flat, picked up my tray and mumbled some incoherent phrase about having to meet someone. Yeah, right. After that embarrassing moment, I felt like a failure and more lonely than before.

A couple of days later, that senior girl came looking for me and knocked on my open door. I invited her in and we sat down to visit. She said that when I approached their table, the young man (with no manners!) was actually breaking up with her. She apologized for her rude behavior and asked if we could have dinner together that night in the cafeteria. We actually became sweet friends and I have looked to her often over the years for wisdom and support.

If you are lonely, instigate a friendship with someone who is lonelier than you are. Listen to someone else's pain and do not talk about your own. The challenge that we all face is that of vulnerability. When you reach out in friendship to someone, you take the risk of being rejected and that is always a possibility. There are few things that are certainties in this life but one of them is this: You will make friends when you become a friend. Satan knows that when you feel alone, he is able to defeat you.

"Then I will strike down the king alone."

- II Samuel 17:2

You can feel lonely without really being alone. We all know married women who ache with loneliness as well as young mothers with houses filled with children who feel alienated and abandoned. We all know popular teenagers who struggle with desperate loneliness. Loneliness is not so much about lacking relationships as it is about building healthy relationships. You will conquer your loneliness when you learn how to give while everyone else is living a self-centered existence. You will no longer feel abandoned if you can learn the secret of being assertively friendly when everyone else is merely passive or by having a cheerful, positive heart when everyone else is uninterested. Remind yourself on a daily basis that love is something that you *do* not something that you feel. If you can reach out in love and kindness to someone every day regardless of how you feel, it will change your life.

The startling truth that I learned during that companionless year in college was that the remedy for my empty heart did not lie in the hands of others, but it had been in my hands all along. Now I remind myself that every day that I am granted another day of living gives me the privilege to reach out in kindness and love to the people that I meet that day. Who knows? My act of generosity or just a smile may be an answer to another's heartfelt prayers. We really do belong to one another and that may be the greatest gift of all!

7

The Problem with People

The good, the bad and the ugly of our emotions! You can either be controlled by your emotions, or you can allow the Holy Spirit within you to control your emotions. You can either vandalize your life with your tongue, or you can allow the Holy Spirit to control your tongue. You can either live a mentally rotten life and allow your thoughts to lay the foundation for negative living, or you can allow the Holy Spirit to clean up your mind. Is it really that easy? I believe that the answer is a resounding, *"Yes!"*

We all have the power of the same Holy Spirit at our access and it is God's will for us all to be filled with the power of that incredible Holy Spirit. Why, then, do some Christian women live with the delightful fruit of joy, peace and patience while others are tormented by not only worry and fear but also anger and frustration? Why do some women use their tongue as an instrument of life and blessing rather than assassinating everyone in their violent path? It is obvious that the peaceful group of women has simply decided to tap into the power of the Holy Spirit in ordinary life situations.

We all tap into the power of the Holy Spirit when we are having our quiet time or listening to a great sermon. But women who have chosen to be controlled by the Holy Spirit 24 hours a day and 7 days a week have given up their flesh and embraced the way of the Spirit. They have unlocked the secret joy of worshiping the Lord both in spirit and in truth. They have been able to transport the power that they experience while in definitive times of praise and worship to become a practical part of their every day life.

Put Your Hand Over Your Mouth

Your heart does not want to be controlled but usually demands to express itself and to ventilate and shout. Whenever I deal with the issues of the heart, I return time after time to this verse:

"The heart is more deceitful than all else."

- Jeremiah 17:9

While your emotional reactions to events and circumstances are threatening to come crashing through the flood gate of your heart, the Holy Spirit is standing right beside your overly emotive heart and just may be jumping up and down, endeavoring to capture your attention, *"Look over here! I am right here! You really can tap into My power! How I would love to flood you with My power right now! Don't say everything you think, feel and believe! Please...don't even say everything that you know!"*

And yet, more often than not, we ignore the voice and the power of the Holy Spirit because we would rather react according to our emotions than allow the Holy Spirit to empower us to respond like Jesus would. It really is possible to tap into the power of the Holy Spirit in these challenging situations and quite frankly, it is not that difficult to do.

When you feel your emotions welling up within you, try quoting the Word of God rather than pontificating and spouting your emotional outrage. Another practical strategy that will help you to harness your boiling estrogen is just choosing to sing a song, either under your breath or right out loud. A method that worked consistently for me when all five of my children were at home was that I would walk out on the front porch, grab the white railing with my white knuckles and just begin to pray for God's power to flood my ugly soul.

Maggot Mouth

"Let no unwholesome word proceed from your mouth, but only such a word as is good for edification according to the need of the moment, so that it will give grace to those who hear. Do not grieve the Holy Spirit of God, by whom you were sealed for the day of redemption."
- Ephesians 4:29-30

We all need to give ourselves practical, Biblical boundaries concerning the words that we allow ourselves to speak. This verse states those boundaries clearly in black and white: We are not allowed to speak anything that is unwholesome. Some translations use the word "corrupt" in place of "unwholesome" though truthfully, neither one of those words communicate the strength of what Paul was trying to say in the original Greek. The word that he used had its root in the Greek word *phaulos*, which refers to something that stinks or is rotting, such as meat that is full of maggots. When you allow your tongue to gossip or wound someone made in the image of Christ, such communication has the stench of decaying trash and it stinks! This type of communication is offensive to the Holy Spirit and it grieves Him.

In Evangelical and Charismatic circles, the phrase, "grieving the Holy Spirit" is spoken with a religious hush. Mistakenly, we believe that grieving the Holy Spirit has to do with how we dress when we attend church or whether or not we tithe to the local church. These verses clearly state that what grieves the Holy Spirit is when we use our tongue as a weapon of mass destruction against people who are made in the image of God.

"The one who guards his mouth preserves his life; the one who opens wide his lips comes to ruin."

- Proverbs 13:3

If you throw open wide that opening between your two lips and verbally vomit on those God has deliberately placed in your life, you are going to decimate many, many relationships that were meant to bring out the best in you. We must always go back to the root of the issue and deal with our hearts.

Imperfect People and Other Problems

My mouth would be a veritable fountain of loveliness and grace if it were not for the people in my world whose job description seems to be performing antics resounding like fingernails on the chalkboard of life. My emotions would be a well-watered garden of beatific blooms, if it were not for people who barge in and ravage my utopian world. Why did God have to ruin the Garden of Eden and create people anyway? People can be ornery and frustrating...they can be stifling and bothersome...and they can be judgmental and critical. People literally do bring out the best in us emotionally or the worst in us emotionally.

People I don't even know personally and will never meet this side of heaven can push my buttons to the extent that I become a raging inferno of bottled up frustration. Who you may ask? Well, I thought that you would never ask, because I can't wait to tell you! People like news anchors who prattle on from their liberal, prejudiced point of view. Who can deal with that biased, opinionated ref who made horrible calls against my favorite basketball team? The nerve of these people who disagree with me! How dare they! My blood pressure begins to rise and my mind is racing in circles and because of these people who are absolute strangers in my life, I justify being short with my husband who merely asked what time dinner would be ready. Or how about that maniac driver in rush hour traffic? I can have on praise and worship music, just singing my little heart out to God when someone cuts in front of me on my way home from work and my peace and joy instantly disappear. I would be a wonderful, nearly perfect woman of God if I never had to have contact with people!

An Inconvenient Ice Storm

My sweet husband, Craig, grew up with his cousin, Kathy, who was really more like a sister to him in many ways. Kathy was exactly 12 months older than Craig and was an only child in a pastor's home. When I married Craig, Kathy and I instantly became best friends, although we are as different as two women can possibly be. She is outspoken and the life of every party while I am more measured in expressing my opinions and would rather spend the night at home with a good book. Kathy is the "take the bull by the horns" kind of girl and I am more a "run away from the bull" kind of girl. Kathy needs me for stabilization and I need her for fun! I would be stagnantly boring without Kathy's unguarded enthusiasm and she would stay in a heap of trouble without my reserve!

Kathy lives in North Carolina, where ice and snow storms do not come often, but when this southern state is attacked by old man winter, every resident of the sun-saturated region rushes to the grocery store to buy milk, bread and eggs. It's always a zoo of wild people, both in the store as they are grabbing up staples and in the parking lot as they endeavor frantically to beat the arctic blast.

Kathy was pregnant and was about to pull into the grocery store parking lot with her teenage son, Adam, so they, too, could purchase groceries to stave off hunger for the next few icy days. Kathy had carefully turned on her blinker and was waiting to pull into the lot out of the traffic pattern when out of nowhere, a hot little sports car spun out in front of her and nearly hit her front fender. The young man seemed to be in a hurry so Kathy gave him the benefit of the doubt this one time and calmly pulled in behind him. (Let me just say, he should have taken the benefit while she was offering it because it wasn't going to last for long.)

He careened down one parking lot aisle while Kathy safely turned into the very next aisle because she didn't want to be anywhere near this madman on ice. She spied a parking place a few cars up and turned on her blinker to claim that spot as her very own. Kathy remarked to Adam that she was so grateful to find a spot close to the front door because pregnant women don't cherish the idea of waddling across the ice. Just as Kathy and her SUV were about to pull into her designated spot, she saw a red flame ignite in her path of vision and that same obnoxious sports car zipped into the parking spot that clearly had her name on it! Kathy laid on her horn and nearly slammed into the back of the car that had practically hit her bumper only minutes before. A young, good-looking, athletic college boy jumped out of the sports car that his daddy had certainly purchased and gave Kathy the…well…let's just say that he wasn't pointing toward heaven as he snickered by Kathy's family vehicle.

Adam was cowering in the passenger's seat in pure terror and begged his mom to just leave and go to another grocery store. Kathy pulled to the end of the parking lot until Mr. College went safely into the grocery store. After he had disappeared from view, Kathy pulled up behind the flaming sports car, extracted her pregnant self out of the driver's seat and calmly let the air out of all four of his sporty little tires. Adam didn't know whether to call 911, his dad, or run for his life!

Kathy pulled into the McDonald's parking lot beside the grocery store and waited for Mr. All American to come out the grocery store doors. She wanted to be somewhere where she could see the action but make a run for it if he spotted her. He had his keys in one hand and a carton of beer in the other hand as he approached his car. He unlocked his door, looked down at his tires and began to heave a string of profanities that would just not be appropriate to repeat in the pages of a book written to Christian women who are trying to learn how to control their emotional impulses. I wouldn't want to give you any new ideas!

Kathy and Adam watched from afar as this impetuous, thoughtless creature did a very unhappy dance right there in the grocery store parking lot. Kathy said that the thought that crossed her mind as she observed this show and tell of tornadic activity was, *Ain't life grand?!*

The Fingerprint of God

Although few of us have ever actually had the nerve to let the air out of someone's tires, we have all certainly had the feelings that Kathy experienced that wintry afternoon. For Kathy, these feelings were directed toward someone she had never met and who will never cross her path again. However, for most of us, the people who know just how to push the right buttons are the people with whom we are in daily relationship. Your dear prince, formerly in shining armor, has fallen off his white steed too many times to count and has left dirty dishes in the sink yet again.

Remember how you used to love those little children that God gave to you? They were so fresh from heaven and you used to breathe in their sweet, newborn smell. Well, you still love them, but forget about smelling them! They have left stinky socks and dirty underwear strewn the length of their bedroom floors with rotten apple cores and half-eaten bowls of cereal underneath their bed frames. And if your 12-year-old son forgets to brush his teeth one more time, he may just find himself moving in with his grandmother!

Sometimes it is the people we love the very most who bring out the extreme worst in us. It is those with whom we are in daily contact who seem to drain us of every bit of Christian virtue until they expose the ugly core of our personality. It's not just family members, but it is the women at work who incessantly gossip until you think you will scream. It is the people at church who whine and complain about every sermon and every decision until you are so frustrated, you wonder if they even know the Lord. It is the neighbors who are rude and the mothers of your children's friends who are completely different than you, and quite frankly, just don't think that you are wonderful.

We all have difficult people in our lives who may have strategically been placed there by God himself. Imagine that! God loves you enough to trust you to be kind to difficult people. God wants you to grow in the fruit of the Spirit and so He allows a boorish, fractious woman to invade the sweet circle of your life. God needs men and women in every generation who will love the unlovable, be kind to the unkind, be patient in the face of ugly impatience and bless those who are categorically cruel.

"You're familiar with the old written law, 'Love your friend,' and its unwritten companion, 'Hate your enemy.' I'm challenging that. I'm telling you to love your enemies. Let them bring out the best in you, not the worst. If all you do is love the lovable, do you expect a bonus? Anybody can do that. If you simply say hello to those who greet you, do you expect a medal? Any run of the mill sinner does that. In a word, what I'm saying is, Grow up! You're kingdom subjects. Now live like it. Live out your God-created identity."

- Matthew 5:43-44, 46–48 The Message

God actually created you to love people who are monstrously rude; He placed you here at this time in history because He trusted that you would indeed mature and then allow His glory to shine out of you into the darkness of people's souls. You will never do this with your own personality or if you rely on the emotional legacy bequeathed upon you by your parents. You will only do this when you determine in your heart that you want to be like Jesus. When you decide that you would rather be like Jesus than like you. When you decide that His way really is better than your way, that you do not have a better idea than God.

"Therefore be imitators of God, as beloved children; and walk in love, just as Christ also loved you and gave Himself up for us, an offering and a sacrifice to God as a fragrant aroma."

- Ephesians 5:1-2

When you demonstrate love in monstrous situations and choose to be kind rather than throw an emotional and well-deserved tantrum, you are saying, "I will act like my Dad! I am part of His family and this is what we do! We love unlovable people. It is the family business to reach out with divine kindness to fractious people." Do not ever forget that you are the beneficiary of the family genetic code that enables you to love difficult people. It is what Christians do!

The world has a different standard of behavior and will encourage you to rationalize rude, vengeful behavior. The world will tell you to spew your feelings out upon difficult people but the world's way has never been God's way. Who do you belong to? The world? Or the Kingdom of God? Perhaps your character, which is revealed when dealing with demanding and critical people, is the litmus test of which kingdom you are actually serving.

When you imitate God and love your husband in spite of his sloppy and insensitive ways, you smell good! When you smile at your ornery neighbor and listen to your loquacious mother, you no longer smell like verbal vomit!

Abusive Tendencies

What about those of you who have genuinely suffered at the mouth and hands of an abuser? Does God call you to sit on your feelings and smile while the abuser is creating damage that will be felt for generations to come? The answer is no. If you are in an abusive relationship, let me simply say this: Jesus does not want you to be abused. Today, go to your pastor or a Christian counselor and develop a plan that will lead you into a healthy life. When I speak of loving difficult people, I am certainly not advocating remaining with those who abuse you emotionally, verbally or physically. There is a gargantuan difference between being frustrated or offended by someone and being abused.

The Power of Prayer

It is been my experience that I am rarely able to "fix" the behavior of challenging people in my life. Responding with emotion to difficult people never produces long-lasting change. I believe that perhaps God has placed you in that difficult person's life not to moderate their irregular behavior, but to pray for them. It is a simple equation that God gives us to deal with those irritable and troublesome hunks of humanity: Love + Prayer = Victory.

"But I say to you, love your enemies and pray for those who persecute you."

- Matthew 5:44

God does indeed have a game plan for every Scrooge, Barney Fife, Cruella DeVille and Simon Cowell that crosses the path of your life. His strategy rarely involves emotion but always has liberal doses of love and prayer mixed together for a victorious conclusion. God did not create you to be some whirling dervish who uses her words to jab, hurt and control people. God created you to be a woman who is more committed to Kingdom than to self. Difficult people can run away from your words, but they can never escape your prayers. We cannot and must not have a disconnect between what we believe and how we treat others, no matter how difficult they may be.

"Let all bitterness and wrath and anger and clamor and slander be put away from you, along with all malice. Be kind to one another, tender-hearted, forgiving each other, just as God in Christ also has forgiven you."

- Ephesians 4:31 & 32

There is an anecdote for bitterness and wrath; it's called kindness. There is a way to overcome anger and clamor; it's known as being tenderhearted. There is also a way to conquer slander; it's recognized as forgiveness.

"Bless those who persecute you; bless and do not curse."

- Romans 12:14

It takes a mature, Godly woman to bless the persecutors in her life. We bless with our tongues, with our heart attitudes, with our emotions and with our actions. Some of you might be thinking, "Yeah, but Carol, you don't know my Aunt Matilda! She is unlovable in every way imaginable!" You may not want to hear my response to your Aunt Matilda scenario but here it is, *Somebody loves your Aunt Matilda and His name is God, so start acting like your Dad!*

We are all unlovable in some way, aren't we? We all can become prickly, outspoken and contentious from time to time, but I believe that the reason most of us are unlovable is because at our very core we are crying out to be loved. There will be many times in life when your decision to love a porcupine will disarm them completely.

The Healing Will Happen to You

Do you have a relationship in your life that needs reconciliation in order for you to become a healthy person emotionally? Maybe your troublesome person has lied to you, cheated you or repeated hurtful gossip about you. The betrayal caused by this person may have penetrated deeply within your soul and your singular thought is, "She doesn't deserve my kindness or my love!" All I can tell you is that I didn't deserve Jesus either and yet He still died for me. You didn't deserve Jesus' love either...so love this person unabashedly! Do it while you are still hurt! Do it regardless of how they respond! Do forgive them completely! Do bless them extravagantly! Just do it!

If you refuse to forgive and then bless the difficult people in your life, you are in danger of becoming a difficult person. The equation is no-fail and will guarantee your eventual victory:

Love + Prayer = Victory!

It's Time for
a Change

Are you in emotional bondage? Are you enslaved to your emotional habits or perhaps to the emotional genetic code that your parents carelessly passed down to you? Many women are cemented to the pain from their past and so are not able to live well in the present. Other women are frustrated with today and feel too hopeless to look ahead. Where do you land on the emotional time line? Do you believe that you can't change no matter how hard you try?

You may rehearse phrases like this as you fall asleep each night: *I know that I shouldn't worry but my gramma worried and my mama worried and I worry, too. It's what we do well! We are champion worriers and there is nothing wrong with that. Some families are musical while others are smart…we just worry well!*

And then you drift off into an often interrupted, restless sleep because you are worrying well.

Perhaps after a particularly testy day filled with unpaid bills, strong-willed toddlers and independent teens, you coddle yourself with these words:

I know that I should not yell at my family, but my parents yelled at me and I turned out perfectly fine. My parents yelled...I yell...and my kids will probably yell, too. Our voices are just louder than most people's voices. It's the only way I can get anyone's attention.

Or, maybe, sadly, this is your repetitive litany:

I can't change. I just can't. I am too old. This is who I am.

This is who I will always be, so just get over it. For once and for all, accept me the way that I am.

Forgive me when I blow it...but don't expect me to change!

Family Movies

One of the most wonderful Christmas gifts that I receive every year is a video that is produced by my teenage daughter, Joni. She creates this annual gift with a compilation of family pictures, videos and memories of each successive year. It is all set to heart touching music that has been especially chosen to make Mama cry. Every Christmas morning, after all of the other gifts have been unwrapped, we gather the family around the television set and the newly pressed DVD is inserted into the DVD player. Even the grandchildren understand that it is a special moment and so each one sits in front of the TV waiting for the "McLeod Family Annual Video."

As soon as the music starts, before even one picture is on the screen, I start crying. It is not just a sweet sob with a single tear or perhaps two running down my unwrinkled yet menopausal cheek, but from the first instant of the introductory note of the yet unidentified melody, I begin to heave. Great, gulping, body-shaking heaves. Usually one of the grandbabies crawls into my lap and snuggles up to my heaving chest and a daughter-in-law or two comes closer to hold my hand as we watch our history unfold before our very eyes.

We watch birthday parties and ball games…we observe graduations and weddings…we tenderly watch pregnant bellies and newborn babies…and we remember those who are no longer with us. At the close of the newly minted DVD, after a moment of applause and laughter, we always begin to talk about how we all have changed.

"Mama! I am so glad that you don't wear your hair like that anymore!"

"Daddy…you sure are more gray than last year!"

"Matt…where did all that hair go?!"

"Jordan…I wish that you would shave your beard again…you are so handsome without facial hair!"

"Can you believe how tall Ian and Wes are getting? Last year they weren't even walking!"

"Olivia! You are so grown up! You are almost a lady!"

"Look how cute Liz looks pregnant! And now she is so skinny!"

"Nanny…you are more beautiful than ever, if that is even possible!"

You, B.C.

Excuse me…but who says you can't change? We change our hair and our size. We change our fashions and the paint on our walls. We lose weight only to gain it back again. We obtain wrinkles and gray hair…and can get rid of both with some Botox and color in a box. Who says you can't change?

We all change, both inwardly and outwardly. The potential for change is one of the greatest possibilities known to mankind. We can change because we can tap into the power of the God who never changes!

"And you were dead in your trespasses and sins, in which you formerly walked according to the course of this world, according to the

prince of the power of the air, of the spirit that is now working in the sons of disobedience. Among them we too all formerly lived in the lusts of our flesh, indulging the desires of the flesh and of the mind, and were by nature children of wrath, even as the rest."

- Ephesians 2:1-3

I would like to point out three extremely significant phrases from this passage of Scripture that will literally rip that "I can't change" rug out from under your glass slippers.

"You were dead ..."
"...in which you formerly walked ..."
"...we too all formerly lived ..."

Something has changed in these verses and that something is you! You have changed! You used to do life one way, but now you have discovered a brand new way of living! Paul is reminding us that "back then" we adhered to a certain way of walking through life, but things are now different. You used to act, talk, react and ventilate in a certain way, but that is all part of your history and not part of your present life. Paul is looking at your old family videos exclaiming, "My, my, my! How things have changed in your life! Are you even the same person any more?"

The Holy Spirit, through the Apostle Paul, is reminding us that we *"formerly walked according to the course of this world."* Girlfriend, you are not who you used to be, so quit acting like the old you! You have changed and you now have the supernatural power to respond differently to situations than you did before Christ. Jesus does indeed have the power to change you! Are you cooperating with Christ and allowing the change to take place in your heart? Or are you continually demanding your own way and defending yourself by saying, "I just can't help it"?

"Walked according to the course of this world" paints a word picture in the Greek that helps us understand why it is indeed a challenge to allow the change to take place inside of our hearts. It is a compound word in the Greek which literally means "to walk around habitually in the same area all the time." But even more than the definition of this word, the grammar structure insinuates that not only did we used to have a bad habit of walking the same ground time after time, but also that it is impossible for us to deviate from this habit and from this particular piece of ground. We were trapped in rotten emotional habits and could not break free from them. We were in bondage to an estrogen-induced coma and were helpless to respond in a healthy way to life's situations and events.

"Indulging the desires of the flesh and the mind" is also an integral part of these verses that help us understand who we used to be. Your emotions used to run rampant and you had no hope of controlling even one of them. When you indulge in or choose to marinate in emotional sludge, you will never be the woman God has created you to be. Our emotions have desires and those desires generally lead us toward some expression of anger. These verses from Ephesians tell us that it is in our human genetic make-up to be the offspring of wrath. Everything that we felt had the same conception point: anger. And then anger gave birth to frustration and unforgiveness; anger begets selfishness and pride; anger's spawn is gossip and bitterness. Before you knew Christ, anger determined your emotional genetic code. That is who you used to be; it is a picture of who you were before you met Christ, but it is not who you are today!

Me? Angry?!

"Be angry, and yet do not sin; do not let the sun go down on your anger, and do not give the devil an opportunity."

- *Ephesians 4:26-27*

I never knew that I had a problem with anger until I became the mother of a two year old. You may laugh or shake your head in incredulity, but it is true. Each woman has a moment in her life when she realizes that the anger virus has not passed her over but that a severe sickness of the soul has broken out in epidemic proportions. For some women, anger rears its ugly head in the teenage years or in marriage as early as the honeymoon. I can guarantee that very few women make it to the years of mothering preschoolers without realizing that anger is not a momentary, light affliction but that it is a plague of the very worst kind.

We all have the propensity to be angry women because without Christ, we have been identified as children of wrath. Jesus knew that there were going to be situations in life that would make us angry and so He spoke to this issue in a very practical way in these verses in Ephesians. Anger is obviously not the sin because this verse says, *"Be angry and yet do not sin..."* It is what you do with the anger that may cause you to sin.

There is a difference between experiencing the emotion of anger from time to time and actually becoming an angry person. In this particular verse, Paul uses two Greek words that when translated literally mean, "a person who brings anger to his side and then embraces it." We all have moments of anger but it is when we allow the anger to become a fundamental component of our personality that the sin begins. The Holy Spirit, through the apostle Paul, is warning the generations of Christians to come that there is a grave danger of developing an intimacy or a closeness with anger. Anger can cause emotional damage that will reverberate for generations if left unchecked. Some of you are the carriers of this emotional gene, while others of you have been the target of this debilitating personality handicap. Every Christian woman needs to do a self-examination from time to time in order to answer this question, *Am I an angry woman?*

Ask yourself these questions and give very honest answers. It would also be appropriate to have someone whom you love and trust answer these questions, as they have observed your life. Self-examinations are never pleasant but the diagnosis is important if you long to live a healthy, peaceful life.

1 – Are my thoughts often critical or negative?

2 – Do my words carry an angry edge?

3 – Is it difficult for me to say encouraging, kind words to people who have been unkind to me?

4 – Has my anger caused relationships to suffer?

5 – Have innocent bystanders become victims of my righteous anger?

6 – Do I often express anger about the little things in life?

7 – Are my angry reactions way out of proportion to the crime?

8 – Do I take anger to bed with me? How often?
    Every night?
    Once a week?
    Once a month?

If you have sinned and taken anger as your lifetime partner, begin the divorce proceedings today! Do not become bedfellows with this devastating partner because the pillow talk that you experience will become lethal.

"And do not give the devil an opportunity."

- Ephesians 4:27

This eight-word sentence found in the powerful Word of God just may be the most practical advice that you have ever received.

The name "devil" in the Greek is the word *diabalos*, which paints a vivid picture of the devil as the "one who repetitiously throws accusations at the mind – striking again and again until he ultimately penetrates the mind with his slanderous lies and relationship-destroying insinuations." (Renner, Rick. 2003. *Sparkling Gems from the Greek.* Tulsa: Teach All Nations. 839.) The devil is irritatingly stupid but he is clever and so is always on the prowl watching your life to see when you have a moment of weakness. For angry people, it is generally at night when they lie in their bed and rather than fellowship with the Lord, they fellowship with their anger. It is at that moment that the devil buys a piece of your emotional real estate.

The word "opportunity" in this phrase is perhaps best translated as an actual geographical place on a map. The devil is looking for a specific place in your life that you have placed on the market so that he has access to everything else that you possess. The devil is out house hunting and is snooping around the boundaries of your life to see if he can place a bid on your peace and your joy. The devil is never able to take anything without our permission and if you are an angry woman, you have given him the keys to your entire life.

The devil would love to enter the safe place of your life and talk to you all night long about your anger. He says things like this as you lay, wide awake, rehearsing your anger:

"You deserve to be angry. That person has never really been kind to you."

"You need to make sure to tell Mary and Anne how Peggy has been treating you, so that they can be careful around her."

"You need to give her a piece of your mind once and for all!"

"No one understands how you have been treated. Just burn your bridges and move on."

However, if rather than reiterate your anger all night long, you would choose to get out of bed and get on your knees, you just might hear God say to you:

"Beloved, just let it go."

"I will give you the strength to forgive and the power to bless!"

"You need My patience and I am pouring it into your life right now."

Sweet Dreams!

God has a purpose for your nighttime hours and it is absolutely not to recite everything and everyone that has angered you over the last three decades. God's purpose for the hours when you are supposed to be sleeping is that He would speak His words and His thoughts into your receptive mind.

"It is vain for you to rise up early, to take rest late, to eat the bread of [anxious] toil; for He gives [blessings] to His beloved in sleep."
- Psalm 127:2 AMP

Extreme Emotional Make-Over

"But God, being rich in mercy, because of His great love with which He loved us, even when we were dead in our transgressions, made us alive together with Christ (by grace you have been saved), and raised us up with Him, and seated us with Him in the heavenly places in Christ Jesus."
- Ephesians 2:4-6

"*But God!*" are two of the most glorious words ever uttered! Into your emotional outrage came God! Into your angry DNA came God! God intervened and rescued you from the relentless habits that held you in bondage. God changed who you were, who you are and the potential for who you will become. When you are frustrated with yourself for the way that you are acting, it would be a good time to cry out, "God, please intervene! Interrupt my emotional sewage with Your loving kindness!"

My name is Carol and I am a word-aholic! I happily confess that I love the way words sound, the way they roll off my tongue and I love all of their various meanings. I am relentlessly on a treasure hunt investigating unique words that I am able to weave into my daily conversations. One of my favorite sites on the Internet is **www.dictionary.com**. I keep this particular site open but minimized on my computer 24/7 so that I am able to easily click on the thesaurus page of the website. (Even now as I tell you about it, my heart is beating rapidly and my blood pressure is rising. I am thrilled to finally be talking about it!) The thesaurus enables me to come up with rare and underused words to replace the ordinary words that I habitually use.

Why use a word like "pretty" when you can use words like "dreamboat" or "beauteous" or "dishy" or "pulchritudinous"?!

Why use an awful word like "awful" when you can say words like "abominable," "ghastly," or even "deplorable"?!

Another addiction that I easily admit to when it comes to being a wordsmith is that I am absolutely fascinated by the new words that are found in the dictionary every year. One year, not long ago, I discovered that these new words were approved to join the classic, overused words in the dictionary:

"unfriend" - the removal of one's friend on a social
networking site
"intexticated" - distracted because of texting on a cell phone while
driving a vehicle
"deleb" - a dead celebrity

Is it contagious? Do you now understand my extreme love for exotic, uncommon and fashionable ways of expressing oneself?

Paul is actually making up words in these three verses because what Christ did for us is so extraordinarily unprecedented that there was no word in the Greek to describe what has happened to you and me. There has been such a revolutionary change in our lives because of God's intervention that Paul conceived three brand spanking-new words to describe the historical event that was instigated due solely to the mercy and love of God.

The first of the new triplet of words is *syzopoieo*, which means "to make alive together with." Have you ever, with your very own eyes, seen someone raised up from the dead? I have to admit that I have not ever seen a miraculous event such as this. I have seen living things die, but I have never seen something brought back to life after dying. Those things just do not happen every day but are known as "miracles"!

You qualify as a living, breathing miracle because you used to be dead and totally unaware of all that Christ accomplished on the cross of Calvary. You were worse than comatose and did not have a clue that God loved you and was offering you the treasure of His great mercy. There was nothing vibrant or active about your life and you were a couch potato of the very worst kind, plodding through life with no purpose or direction. You were truly the walking dead. You were a zombie rife with decay, particularly concerning your moral and emotional state. When suddenly, God came to your rescue and threw you the Life Line of all life lines and now you are no longer the walking dead but you are actively getting better and better!

You have fresh power and a meteoric way of dealing with not only your thinking, but also with your emotions and your personality. You are no longer in bondage to that ridiculous pony ride at the fair but are going through life in an entirely different direction with a spring in your step.

Before you knew Jesus, when something happened to frustrate you or upset you, you would turn in the only direction that you knew, which was toward anger and all of its ugly children. But now, because you gloriously know Christ, when something happens to upset the apple cart of your life, you are able to turn toward love and forgiveness. When you do not get your own way, you don't throw a fit but you enter into worship. When a tragic or traumatic event slams into your life, you are not decimated but continue to trust the God of all hope. At its very core, the definition of a Christian is someone who has been changed by the power of Christ and so responds to life differently.

Say it loud and say it strong: *I have been syzopoeieoed!* (If Paul can make up new words, well then, so can I!)

The second of the triplet of words that Paul has conceived is the Greek word *synegeiro*, which means "to raise up with Christ." Paul actually models this word after the word that was used to describe the ascension of Jesus Christ. Paul is desperately trying to communicate with the church at Ephesus and with every generation of Christians to come that we were raised up, not to live a life of mere humanity, but that we were raised up to literally live a heavenly life while still breathing in the atmosphere of planet earth. Because we have been *"synegeiro-ed,"* we are living a new and blessed life that is entirely devoted to God. Why, then, do we honk our horns in standstill traffic, yell at the sales clerk who gives us the wrong change, or give our husbands the silent treatment? My sisters, these things ought not to be so!

All of our emotional decisions are now made with eternity's goals in mind and so no longer do we ask the question, "How can I tell her how I feel?" But rather the question becomes, "How do I express God's love in this situation?"

We are no longer consumed with manipulating and controlling so that we get our own way, but we are consumed with the possibility of bringing heaven's atmosphere to earth's problems. Our lives are no longer about self or emotional outrage because we have been raised up and are above the bondage of earth's value system. We see things differently because of the vantage point of being raised up. Because I am looking down on my problems and not horizontally at them, I am no longer consumed with self or even sadness, but I am determined to usher the presence of Christ into all of my life's situations.

Now you need to declare with Paul, with the church at Ephesus and with me, *I have been synegeiroed!*

The third of the triplet of words that Paul gave birth to is the word *synkathizo*, which means that you are seated right beside Christ. You have been given the very best seat in the entire house as you travel through life. You have a heavenly perspective and thus the point of view of Christ. You will see your life as He sees your life and He will be coaching you through it every step of the way.

When I fly, I love the airlines that provide a small television screen on the back of the seat in front of me. I quickly flip through the available channels and skip over the soap operas, news channels, sporting events and cartoons because I have one channel in mind. I love the station that provides the satellite picture of exactly where your plane is as you fly over the surface of the earth. This channel actually provides the information of how fast the plane is traveling, what the altitude of the plane is and precisely where we are. I am delighted to know that I am over Iceland or the Rocky Mountains or the Gulf of Mexico.

This is what being *"sinkathizo'ed"* does for you. You have heaven's perspective on earth's situations! You have God's vantage point of your life and you are able to see clearly what He is trying to develop in you and in the people in your pathway.

I have been sinkathizo'ed!

9

The Blahs

You might be a completely mature Christian woman who has overcome anger and worry. You may not even have a lingering memory over the days when you struggled with fear, loneliness or depression. However, even the godliest of women deal with this next challenge. This totally benign issue hits all of us from time to time. It is not a permanent emotional disability and usually we think of it as, "Here today...gone tomorrow!"

The blahs. What exactly are the blahs? This headache of the soul cannot truly be defined as "depression" because you are still able to function if you have been targeted by the blahs. You are still choosing – however lethargically – to place one foot in front of the other. You are still able to interact with people, although your answers are not quite as scintillating or vibrant. You have not retreated into a cave yet although languishing underneath an afghan, a long nap and complete quiet sure are tempting. Every day. All day.

You are still able to do the dishes. *Sigh*. You can still pay the bills. *Double sigh*. And you probably will get around to going to the grocery store. *Yawn*.

You are able to get up every morning, although you only function at half of your potential. You are not depressed, but neither are you joyful or excited about anything at all. Day after day come and go in a vacuum of gray nothingness. You smile now and then but it never goes all the way to your heart. Your get up and go...got up and went. Somewhere. You are just not sure where it got up and went to!

The victim of the blahs is generally yanked back into reality by some event such as a women's conference, a friend's attention or a vacation. Then, once again, life looks sunny and the blahs have been swept back under your emotional carpet for another year or two.

Knowing that the blahs are not long-lasting and that you are still able to function at a mediocre level, what is so wrong with entertaining them? Is it a sin? The blahs usually don't do any long-term damage...or do they? The blahs don't inhibit you from teaching Sunday School...although they might sap your creativity. The blahs don't paralyze you from cooking a meal every night...although you might eat an extra serving or two of dessert.

1440

Every night when the clock strikes midnight, you don't turn into a pumpkin but you are the recipient of a brand new, shining gift. We all receive the same amount of this gift regardless of weight, age, education, beauty, job description or marital status. When each new day raises its sleepy head, you are the sole owner of 1440 of the most powerful commodity ever known in the history of mankind. At precisely one second after midnight, every single day of your life, heaven opens its windows and gives to you 1440 untouched and valuable minutes to spend. How you spend your minutes is entirely up to you! Time is free, but it is priceless!

You can gossip or you can worship…you can be filled with anger or with gratitude…you can jog five miles or watch television all day long…you can read a book or go to the mall. You, and you alone, choose how you will capitalize on this extravagant and priceless gift. You can choose to laugh or to cry…to whine or rejoice…to be negative or to be positive…to be bitter or to be better. These 1440 pieces of time belong to you and to no one else but you! They are not your husband's or your boss's or your children's to spend.

Now, because I can read women's minds, I know what you might be thinking:

"Wait just a minute, Carol! People place all sorts of demands upon my life! I must work and take out the trash. If I don't do the laundry and go to the grocery store, my family won't eat and we will all wear dirty clothes!

"I have to take care of my aging parents, pay the bills and take little Benjamin and Betty to piano and soccer and gymnastics.

"Most of my 1440 are spent for me! Everyone else cashes my time check, helps themselves liberally to every moment that has been given to me until, quite frankly, I am in the red when it comes to time! It's all gone before I make any choices at all! I need more than 1440!

I need 1880, or 2020 wouldn't be bad, either!"

Take a deep breath and allow me to respond, because it is true that there are things that we have to do. Most of us must work, but we choose *how* we work. We can either go to the office with a chip on our shoulder, filled with angst and negativity or we can walk in with a happy heart, a solid work ethic and praying for those in our office. You can hate every minute that you are at work and waste time by gossiping with the girls in the office, playing computer games and sneaking out the door five minutes early. Or you can know that God has set you in this particular office to be a blessing and to bring the excellence and character of God into your workplace.

It is true, you have to take care of aging parents, raise your children and take out that dreaded trash. Nevertheless, you choose *how* to do your *have-to's*. You can march through life with heavy steps and a frustrated heart or you can perform all of the necessities in life with patience, love and joy.

Things I Love!

My mother knows how to make a grand entrance and several years ago, the entrance that she made into my home for Easter weekend was one of the grandest of all. She arrived at my house on Good Friday afternoon with eight boxes of goodies from the Amish Bakery. I am not exaggerating. Eight boxes filled with blueberry pie, pumpkin bread, peanut butter cookies, coconut cake, and pecan rolls were only the beginning of the Easter Parade of desserts. I could feel the pounds packing on as I merely sniffed the delicious mounds of sugared confections that were placed on my kitchen counter.

She also ushered in two shopping bags filled with her used, designer purses and wondered if either I or my daughters and daughters-in-law would enjoy them. Enjoy them? Designer purses that had only been used once or twice?! Let us at them!

In addition to the two shopping bags filled with designer purses, she also brought three shopping bags packed to the rim with shoes, still in their boxes, that had never been worn. My mom has a delightful habit of buying shoes one half size too small for her feet but that miraculously fit mine! It works for me!

She handed all of the boys who were at home a $20 bill and

gave to each of the girls a piece of heirloom jewelry. As I said, my mom knows how to make quite the entrance.

After we each had a peanut butter cookie straight from the heart of Amish country, the matriarch of our family gathered us all around the granite countertop in my kitchen. She said that she wanted to read something to us that she had written that day while on the five-hour car trip from her home to ours. We all obediently gathered and the family grew quiet because we had learned that when Mimi speaks, y'all better listen now, ya' hear?!

She drew a piece of paper from out her designer purse and read us the title, "Things I Love" and then made us all listen to things that she loves. Because I had to listen to Mom's list…so do you! It might just cure you of your case of the blahs!

Things I Love

Hot Baths
Two year olds
Houses on Hills
Pretty Hair-Dos
Laughter
Chocolate
Children Who Rave About Their Parents
(I think that there was a subconscious message in this one!)
Yellow Daffodils
Hometowns
Lattes
Pumpkin Pie
Lines in the Carpet (She is a clean-aholic!)
Luxurious Vacations
Happy Husbands

Sparkling Windows
Rides in the Country
Sunday Afternoons
Positive People
Love Stories
Diamonds
Blue Skies
Old Ladies (Of which she is most certainly NOT one!)
Picturesque Churches
Immaculate Houses
Purses (Who could have guessed?!)
Loyal Friends

There is not a blah bone in my mother's 70-something-year-old body! She has learned the life lesson well that every day is meant to be enjoyed and celebrated. Her life has not been perfect nor uneventful, but she carries a song in her soul and sings it loudly.

God's Anecdote to the Blahs

"This is the day the LORD has made; we will rejoice and be glad in it."

- Psalm 118:24 (NKJV)

This is your daily game plan and guaranteed life strategy to beat the blahs. Every day that has been generously given to you by the Lord is a new opportunity to manage your day with praise. This is one of the most familiar scriptures in the entire Bible and yet we overlook its importance and ignore its possibilities. God gave you this day and designed it especially with you in mind. He has a plan for you every single day of your life that always includes a liberal dose of praise. If you want the assurance that you are participating in God's will for your life on a daily basis, it is vital that you start your day with praise, that you fill it with worship and that you end it with thanksgiving. From the first moment of consciousness to your last waking thought at night, make it a choice of your will to only magnify the Lord and never question Him. We are not a people who blame the Lord, we are a people who bless the Lord!

These are your minutes... all 1440 of them... so spend them well. Spend them on something of importance and something that actually matters. This day will never come again and a day that is given to the blahs is never returnable. When you give a day of your very short life to the blahs, you have just wasted 1440 pieces of pure gold.

Rejoicing is an act of your will and you must choose to do it. There will be days when the worship just instinctively wells up within you and a bastion of the blahs would not be able to hold it back. But there will be many more days when you must choose to rejoice and command yourself to whistle a happy tune. There will be weeks when you must command yourself to sing or utter words of thanksgiving out loud.

"Bless the LORD, O my soul, and all that is within me, bless His holy name. Bless the LORD, O my soul, and forget none of His benefits."
- Psalm 103:1-2

David was a common man with an uncommon heart. He struggled with emotional outrage, just as you and I do. He stood on the edge of the black pit of depression times too numerous to count and thus, he knew what it took to battle the blahs as well. David chose to command his soul, which is the birthplace of our thoughts, emotions and personality, to bless the Lord. This phrase is constructed in the imperative, which means that it is not an option but a definitive command. David was, in effect saying, "Soul, no matter how crummy you feel, you will bless the Lord! Personality, get over yourself and praise the Lord! Now! Emotions, shut your whining, complaining mouth and open up to worship the Lord!"

Praise will reform the atmosphere of your life in a way that nothing else has the power to do. There is one person and one person alone who keeps you from rejoicing. You might try to blame it on the devil but he does not have the power to inhibit your heart from breaking into song. The devil actually has realized that he doesn't need to mute your ability to worship because this other person has done such a thorough job that the devil's devious ways are no longer needed. Who is this powerful inhibitor that stands between you and the symphonic explosion of worship? You! You do! You choose not to rejoice when you are consumed with the not-so-benign blahs.

There is really only one reason why a Christian who loves Jesus wholeheartedly would choose not to rejoice. There is one reason that can be expressed in an infinite number of ways. Selfishness. Self-centered living. Self-awareness. Looking out for #1! Self-preservation. My way or the highway. Life is all about me. I don't feel like it. I don't gotta if I don't wanna.

It is your choice. You choose to magnify self today or to magnify God. Choose today.

"Let those be clothed with shame and dishonor who magnify themselves over me."

- Psalm 35:26

When you are more consumed with self than you are with God, your life will have a putrid shame about it. There will be a vile odor that emanates from all of your decisions, all of your thoughts and all of your heart attitudes. When you focus more on your desires and preferences than on the Word of God, you are choosing an ugly, outdated wardrobe. It's like going to the thrift store and telling the sales lady, "Give me the most hideous outfit in the store and I will wear it out of here proudly!" That is how you choose to outfit yourself emotionally when you decide not to worship because in some type of warped, prejudiced justification you don't *"feel"* like it.

You dishonor the God who made you in His own image when you think about "you" more than you think about Him! You disrespect the Brother who gave His own life for you so that you could not only live eternally after death, but also live abundantly today!

"Sing for joy in the LORD, O you righteous ones; Praise is becoming to the upright."
- Psalm 33:1

If your desire is to become the lovely woman that God intended for you to be, you will then determine in your heart that even on the grayest of days you will praise Him! If you long to be the very best version of yourself in all of life's situations, then your heart will break out in praise regardless of the events or circumstances in your life. Praise is not an event-driven activity but it is a response to the God of all creation and to Him whose very nature is love. He remains the same although your circumstances change therefore, He deserves your highest praise on chemo days, on divorce days and on blah days. If you choose not to worship Him because of disappointing events or devastating circumstances, you are denying yourself not only the victory that He longs to lead you toward, but you are also refusing the beauty that He is offering to you.

When you choose to sing rather than to whine, the atmosphere of your life is transformed. People perceive you differently when you make this imperative choice of the soul. You will become more becoming in every way imaginable. The ugliest version of you is the selfish, whining version; the most beautiful portrayal of who God imagined that you would be happens when you worship.

Kathy Strikes Again

Kathy, the delightful combustion of energy, opinion and joy, not only lets the air out of aggravating people's tires, but in her free time she is a nurse at a very prestigious medical center in the south. Remember meeting Kathy in Chapter Seven? If you don't, take my word for it, you need to go back and read that chapter again!

Kathy has been a nurse at Duke University Medical Center for nearly three decades. For most of these years, she has served in the intensive care unit for newborn babies. Infants are placed in this critical care unit due to debilitating conditions caused either by premature birth, serious illness or by the exposure to drugs or alcohol while in the mother's womb. Currently, Kathy is a specialized lactation consultant and helps with not only the feeding process in the early days of an infant's life but also with the bonding process between mother and high needs baby.

Kathy has often told me that although each baby comes with a story and each story is equally heartbreaking, that the saddest cases of all are babies who are diagnosed with FTT or failure to thrive. These particular babies just don't gain weight and have lost their will to live. They are not hitting all of the significant milestones that babies are supposed to encounter on their way to toddlerhood. It is an extremely common diagnosis among children who are brought up in orphanages or in homes where they are not held nor stimulated. FTT happens when the child, or even an infant, realizes that he or she is merely a number or a case study and not the beloved of any parent.

This is what Kathy has to say from a clinical point of view concerning failure to thrive:

Failure to thrive is the inability to sustain life. Many infants, for numerous reasons, are diagnosed with this condition. The most common reason for this diagnosis in full term infants is the lack of food. Mothers water down the baby's formula or feed them less than 6-8 times per day. Sometimes, parents ignore the gastrointestinal issues the child may be exhibiting. Education is a major factor in helping parents realize that their child needs more food than is being offered. Other reasons for this condition may include malabsorption of nutrients, premature infants who have not yet developed a mature intestinal system or babies born with congenital defects that impair their nutrition.

It is important to realize that there is a clinical explanation for failure to thrive, as well as an emotional explanation. Kathy continues to explain, from her heart, what the emotional cause and consequences of failure to thrive include:

The biggest reason we see failure to thrive across the world, however, is lack of personal skin-to-skin bonding. Infants in orphanages across the world experience this condition at alarming rates because they are left in cribs for most of their infant days and are held rarely. These babies have learned not to cry to be held and are often viewed as "good" babies. Eventually these babies cannot metabolize their food, therefore they lose interest in it and they die.

Kathy's true passion, birthed from years of observing mothering techniques and bonding issues with both healthy newborns and high needs infants, embraces not only nutrition issues, physical limitations and foreign challenges but also the mistakes of our advanced culture:

Our country, America, is quickly heading in this same direction on a less obvious level. Human beings are a carrying species, not a nesting species. American baby product companies are coming out with every possible product to enable us NOT to hold our babies. Even some well-intentioned Christian books are written from the perspective that it will spoil your infant if you hold them rather than let them cry. Holding, cuddling and skin-to-skin contact are all mandatory for his/her physical well being and mental health issues. Skin-to-skin contact, as seen every three hours with breastfeeding mothers (referred to as Kangaroo Care in Neonatal Units), is as important as the food itself to the infant.

When infants are placed upon his or her mother's chest and their hearts are in proximity, the mother's core body temperature will go up to warm the infant. Her body will cause the infant's heart rate to regulate, his respirations to become normal and it will regulate the infant's temperature. This Intelligent Design is perfect...not to mention the perfect nutrition offered by the breast, which happens to be next to the mother's heart.

Failure to thrive babies who are healthy enough to survive infancy, grow up to be children who are never comfortable being touched, if they were never held or caressed as infants. The damage is irreparable without divine intervention. Even if these babies live, they have still suffered from a tragic and real death: the death of who they could have been if they had merely been held during their earliest formative days.

Y.O.U. And F.T.T.

I am sure that by now you are wondering how Kathy's opinions, however well researched, intersect with your inability to overcome the blahs. How does this discussion of failure to thrive translate to a spiritual application? The truth is, if you are spending even one day a month marinating in the blahs, you, too, my friend are suffering from FTT. The diagnosis is obvious: you are spiritually listless, have no energy and are stunted from growing in your faith.

Perhaps you are being fed watered-down spiritual nutrients or are not being fed often enough. Or, it is possible that due to heart attitudes such as bitterness, anger or unforgiveness that you are unable to absorb the meat of the Word.

"Therefore, putting aside all malice and all deceit and hypocrisy and envy and all slander, like newborn babies, long for the pure milk of the word, so that by it you may grow in respect to salvation, if you have tasted the kindness of the Lord."

- I Peter 2:1-3

For some of us, our blahs reflect the lack of "skin-to-skin" bonding with the Lord; an ignoring of the intimacy that Christ longs to experience with each one of us. This skin-to-skin contact is absolutely possible, even though we serve a God who lives in heaven while we live and breathe on planet earth. The Word is the tangible evidence of His presence and so spending time in the Word of God will increase your capacity to develop a thriving attitude toward life. The Psalmist tells us that God inhabits the praises of His people and so when you enter with reckless abandon into a time of worship, you are the beneficiary of spirit-to-spirit contact with the God of the universe! I guarantee that worship will throw the blahs out the door and welcome His presence into your life. You will flourish in every way and the blahs will now be part of a foreign vocabulary. When we bond with the Lord by resting in His presence, it is then that His heart regulates our lives.

We are not a nesting species because our hearts long to be carried by our Heaven Father. Our culture has offered a veritable smorgasbord of counterfeit options that vie to replace the security only our Father's arms can offer. We have allowed materialism and education to usurp time spent in His presence. We have made room for entertainment and recreation and yet have found no room for Him in the inn of our hearts.

"Surely I have composed and quieted my soul; like a weaned child rests against his mother, my soul is like a weaned child within me."
- Psalm 131:2

Do not ever take for granted those solitary moments spent in the presence of the Savior of your soul. These moments which quickly turn into hours are among the most vital that you spend every day of your existence. You will never thrive, nor flourish, nor become the creature of beauty that God meant for you to be unless you, too, quiet your soul upon your Father's chest. We are easily swayed into believing that we can exist without intimacy but the resounding truth of medical research, sociological statistics and spiritual certainty is that we will never thrive without time spent in heart-to-heart contact with our heavenly Father. Please do not fool yourself into believing that you are immune to spiritual FTT because it can happen to all of us far more quickly than we can imagine. If we are not in daily communion with Jesus, we can rapidly lose hope and begin to falsely believe that life has no intrinsic meaning. Failure to thrive is not the presence of diagnosed mental illness or clinical depression, but it is the absence of mental vigor and emotional vivaciousness.

Craig and I have a plaque that is strategically placed by our front door:

"The glory of God is a human being fully alive; and to be alive consists in beholding God."

— *Saint Iranaeus*

The words of this great man of God echo significantly and resoundingly through nearly 2,000 years of church history. Human beings were created to reveal the glory of God, not to exhibit a paralysis of spirit. We are most alive when we are spending time listening for the heartbeat of the One who created us, loves us and shares His glory with us.

Marinate in What?!

I am not a vegetarian but I could easily become one because I rarely eat meat due to…well…because I really don't like the way meat tastes most of the time. I think that meat is too pungent and wild-tasting and beyond that, I hate touching raw meat. Yuck! My gag reflex is beginning to kick in just writing about my opinion on anything carnivorous.

I tolerate chicken and some fish, but scarcely ever do I eat salmon or red meat. I can delight my palate with a variety of other food groups such as chocolate…and carbs…and desserts. I have always felt that a well-balanced meal is a Snickers bar and a Diet Coke. What's wrong with that?

A few summers ago, our youngest daughter, Joni, and I spent nearly two weeks with our oldest son, Matt, his wife, Emily and my delightful granddaughter, Olivia. Emily eats things like hummus and gluten-free bread, not to mention the fact that she also runs at least five miles a day. She has her family on much the same regimen so going to her house is always like a crash diet for me. It never fails – I always come home from Matt and Emily's very organic house at least five pounds lighter than when I walked in their front door. Her cooking style and nutritional choices are nothing short of miraculous to me because I am the mother-in-law who orders take-out at least three nights a week and it ain't organic, if you know what I mean!

Emily told me one afternoon during our stay at her house, that we were going to have salmon on the grill for dinner that night. I swallowed hard and smiled and said, "Anything that you make will be great!" Hey…I was telling the truth! I knew that it would be great FOR me but I wasn't so sure how great my taste buds would like it!

I noticed that in usual Emily-style, she was pouring and dumping a various display of ingredients together in a bowl in the kitchen. I stayed in the living room and enjoyed building blocks with Olivia while at the same time plotting mentally, *I wonder if I can make a grocery store run after Olivia goes to bed tonight and sneak some ice cream into this house?*

And then I had another ominous thought, *Oh no! But this is Emily! I wonder if there is some kind of sugar-alarm that goes off if you walk in the door with anything not on her all-organic, all-natural, never-been-processed, nearly vegetarian, it's-gotta-be-good-for-you list?*

I wasn't willing to chance an alarm going off, so I knew that I would need help: I would need to enlist the services of my progeny, Matthew, who also had a near addiction to carbs, sugar and processed food.

By now, Emily had come back into the living room and joined Olivia and me in our attempt to build a tower of only-pink blocks. I innocently asked if there was anything I could do to help her get ready for dinner. She assured me that everything was ready to go and that the salmon was marinating in the refrigerator.

Marinating?! Salmon marinates? I thought incredulously to myself. *I not only have to choke down that foul-tasting fish but I wonder what it is soaking in? Perhaps tofu? Or split-pea soup?*

When we all sat down to dinner that night, Emily served each one of us a plate filled with exotic, healthy wonders. We were each offered a green salad sprinkled with feta cheese and a homemade vinaigrette, and a sweet potato that was artfully cut in two and garnished with cinnamon. But the centerpiece on every plate was that oh-so-anticipated salmon that had been marinated in heaven knows what!

I kept my napkin ready in my hand in case I needed to quickly wipe my mouth and secretively spit something out into the aforementioned napkin. We were smiling and talking and while the attention was on Olivia for something cute that she had just said, I gingerly placed a piece of the mystery-marinated salmon in my mouth. Did I mention that it was a very, very small piece? I fully expected my eyes to water and my gag reflex to kick in when suddenly I detected the delightful taste of a vinegary sweetness mixed with my favorite soy sauce and topped off with a delectable herb dill. The salmon was incredible! It was absolutely fabulous! 4-Star in every way imaginable!

"Emily!" I exclaimed. "You have outdone yourself with this salmon! It is beyond incredible…truly the best salmon I have ever tasted! What did you do with it?"

My sweet daughter-in-law looked at me with a grin on her face and said, "I had a feeling that salmon wasn't your favorite thing in the world to eat so I remembered the spices and flavors that you did enjoy and made a marinade for the fish. I knew that the salmon would take on the flavor of whatever it was marinating in and so I did it just for you."

Did you hear that? Allow me to quote my brilliant and healthy daughter-in-law: *"I knew that the salmon would take on the flavor of whatever it was marinating in and so I did it just for you."*

This culinary principle translates into our emotional and spiritual choices as well: you will take on the flavor of whatever it is in which you choose to marinate. If you spend time thinking critical, negative and bitter thoughts then you will become a critical, negative and bitter woman. If you spend all of your extra hours shopping, redecorating your home, and spending money then you will become a shallow, materialistic woman. But if you choose to marinate yourself in the presence of God for as long as possible every day of your life, you will become a woman who is filled to overflowing with vitality, emotional health and the peace of heaven.

God's recipe for a tasty, delightful life is that you would not waste one day marinating in the blahs but that you would grow in joy and kindness every day of your life. You will only do that when you place yourself in His presence and rest there. If you do not marinate in the presence of God, the rest of your world will be missing out on the gift that God has offered to them because you are a part of their lives. Your main job in life is to stay connected to God and to marinate in all that He has and all that He is. In His presence, there are no blahs but only the fullness of joy!

Back to 1440

Remember? You have been given 1440 miraculous minutes every day in which to bear fruit and worship the Lord. The cure for the blahs is magnifying the Lord and dying to self. Understanding the power of the 1440 means that no matter what I am doing – whether it is the laundry, grocery shopping, taxiing my children or fixing dinner – I am rejoicing!

What is the greatest tragedy in life? Is it cancer or death? Is it bankruptcy or losing your home? I believe that the greatest tragedy in life is being alive without joy!

If you live to be 80 years old and use your 1440 every day to honor God and serve people, you will still discover that is a very small slice in eternity.

"He has made everything beautiful in its time. He has also set eternity in the hearts of men; yet they cannot fathom what God has done from beginning to end."

- Ecclesiastes 3:11 (NIV)

I have heard it said that none of us is allowed to choose the day we will die but all of us have the option of choosing how we will live the days that we have been given. 1440 is all yours! The next time that the grayness of the blahs knocks at the front door of your heart, don't answer! Put your hands in the air and start to worship! Remind yourself that today is a gift and you will use it while marinating in His presence!

Disappointments, Broken Hearts and Other Maladies of the Soul

Did you know that there is a difference between disappointment and a broken heart? One of the most devastating consequences of being an estrogen-saturated woman is that it becomes very difficult to distinguish between a temporary disappointment and the trauma of a truly broken heart. When a woman with little emotional stability deals with a disappointment, she makes the crucial mistake of labeling it as a broken heart. Both disappointment and broken hearts are genuine and sobering, but they are also light years apart in consequence. Most of the Christian women I know, and that includes me, have at one time, misinterpreted a disappointment as a broken heart.

"Seeing that His divine power has granted to us everything pertaining to life and godliness ..."

- II Peter 1:3

Really?! Everything?! Everything that I will ever need as long as I am living has been granted to me by His divine power? That seems nearly too good to be true! What this "wow" scripture communicates is that there is not one situation in life that God's power is not able to help you handle. His power is able to assist you in keeping your disappointments in their proper perspective and also comforts you when you have suffered a broken heart. It's nothing short of miraculous.

Disappointment vs. Broken Hearts

It seems like everywhere you look, there are painful reminders that many people indeed suffer from a broken heart and it colors every system of their lives. A broken heart may change the way that you think and process information and also has the potential to affect the way that you are able to interact with other human beings. A broken heart certainly has the power to determine that all other emotions are only to be sung in a minor key.

A broken heart is usually caused by some catastrophic event, such as the death of a child or a painful divorce. Some women's broken hearts are caused by a lifetime of singleness or infertility. For others, it is dealing with the agony of rebellious children or the reality that life is passing by rapidly and failure is the only legacy that you are leaving.

May I just gently remind you that there is a difference between a broken heart and disappointment? Do not turn your disappointments into a broken heart; do not give them that kind of power in your life. Keep your disappointments in their proper perspective.

College Woes

It was the end of my junior year in college and I had dated a certain young man on and off for nearly two years. I cared for him deeply but still was not quite sure if he was "the one" or not. He was a leader and I liked that; he was smart and I liked that even more; he was witty and outgoing and I thoroughly enjoyed his company.

One spring day, I saw him in the cafeteria with another girl and I could tell instantly that he wasn't merely meeting with her for a benign homework assignment. I knew by the look on his handsome face that he was deeply involved in a lingering conversation with the beautiful nursing major. My heart stopped and I knew immediately that I was in trouble. Big trouble of the heart.

Later that same day, I saw them together in his 1970 white Impala. Sheila was sitting close to him in a spot that I had thought was reserved only for me. I turned away from the romantic twosome and hightailed it for my college dorm room. With dramatic flair that only a young woman in the throes of rejection is able to conjure up, I threw myself upon my turquoise bedspread and began to weep. I was the object of injustice and rejection. My young heart was broken into at least two pieces, and I sobbed great heaving sobs.

My roommate cautiously entered the room and found me lying in a puddle of tears, a pile of soggy tissues and self-righteous outrage. Debby compassionately sat beside me, began to rub my back and tenderly asked what was wrong. I told her through ample tears and gulps, every detail of my horrible day.

"Carol, do you trust God or not?" she wisely asked me. "You had asked God whether or not he was the one for you and God has just answered your prayer. Now, let me take you out to lunch!"

Believe me when I say that he was not the man for me. God actually saved me from having a broken heart by allowing me to walk through, in retrospect, a very minor disappointment.

Disappointment

So many things in life disappoint us. I am daily disappointed by the weather, the sports teams for which I cheer, the prices at the mall and the stock market. Some of you are disappointed by your husbands, your children's grades, the mail that is delivered to your house and the meal that you ordered at your favorite restaurant. If you allowed yourself to do so, you could spend a large portion of every day of your life dealing with the disappointment that someone or something has thrown your way. Disappointment could easily become the color of our lives, due to the people and events that never quite meet our high expectations.

"And not only this, but we also exult in our tribulations, knowing that tribulation brings about perseverance; and perseverance, proven character; and proven character, hope; and hope does not disappoint, because the love of God has been poured out within our hearts through the Holy Spirit who was given to us."

- Romans 5:3-5

The apostle Paul, the writer of the book of Romans, gives us a better way to handle disappointments than being disappointed. What Paul is patiently teaching in this tactically important passage of Scripture is that disappointments do not have the power to disappoint you! God has appointed you for goodness and for destiny, therefore disappointments have no power to undo what God has already done. When we become emotionally stressed out and frustrated due to the daily disappointments in life, we are giving each disappointment too much authority in our lives. One of the greatest keys in dealing with disappointments is to keep them in their proper perspective.

To "dis-appoint" means that your destiny has been forever changed; that once you were appointed for destiny and significance but that the disappointing event has forever altered your eternal purpose. "Dis-appointment" would imply that once you were appointed and that some circumstance has stolen your appointment. Daily occurrences or events do not have the authority to dis-appoint you from God's appointment for you!

Paul instructs the Body of Christ for all generations to come, that our response to disappointments should be wholehearted exultation. The King James Bible translates this verse using an incredible word, "...*we glory in tribulations, also ...*"

We have had it all wrong! We have mistakenly believed that tribulations, or disappointments, are tragic, life-altering obstacles, when the Bible, which is our compass into all Truth, tells us that disappointments are our finest hour. It is the opportunity that Christians have to show that we, indeed, are different and that we take this moment to reveal the glory that has been placed within us. We don't cry because of disappointments, we rejoice in them. We don't wail due to disappointments, but we look for the fingerprint of God to reveal itself.

"I didn't get the promotion? That's ok because God is still
God and I am still worshipping! He is my Provider!"
"My child didn't win the scholarship? God is my Source!
I will not worry but I will trust!"
"My husband forgot to take out the trash? Not a problem...
I will do it for him and fix his favorite dinner tonight!"

The reason that we are able to rejoice, Paul says, is because we know that the hard stuff in life turns us into the right stuff. Paul tells us to get excited! Get very excited about your trial because it is going to turn you into something better than you could have been without the trial. You are about to become a woman of perseverance who no longer throws a temper tantrum when she doesn't get her way. Perseverance is the ability to face difficulties without giving in emotionally to the difficulties.

"And not only this, but we also exult in our tribulations, knowing that tribulation brings about perseverance ..."

- Romans 5:3

I've got good news for you...and I've got bad news for you. Which do you want first? I think that I will give you the good news first: When you encounter a trial, you become a better version of you! You become a woman who has the spiritual tenacity to walk powerfully through the storms of life. Yea, God! Yea, you! If you can learn the secret of revealing the glory of God inside of you during the most difficult days of your life, you will become a woman of strength and valor.

Now for the bad news...perseverance is not the end goal of going through difficult situations in life. It is merely step one in this arduous journey that will only be conquered by placing one foot in front of the other and keeping your eyes on Jesus. Perseverance now points you toward proven character.

"And not only this, but we also exult in our tribulations, knowing that tribulation brings about perseverance; and perseverance, proven character..."

- Romans 5:3-4

It is always interesting to read how various translations of the Bible translate a singular portion of Scripture. Let's take a look at several different translations of this same phrase from Romans 5:3-4:

"We can rejoice, too, when we run into problems and trials, for we know that they help us develop endurance. And endurance develops strength of character ..." (NLT)

"And not only so, but we also rejoice in our tribulations: knowing that tribulation worketh steadfastness; and steadfastness, approvedness ..." (ASV)

But I think that the King James Version is the one that I am most able to apply to my life:

"And not only so, but we glory in tribulations also: knowing that tribulation worketh patience; and patience, experience ..."

If you have never before encountered a trial or a tribulation, you are an inexperienced, wet-behind-the-ears Christian. But, if you have rejoiced your way through a tribulation and found a strength that you never before had, now you are one experienced girl! And you know what experience will get you...experience will always get you the job! If you are one of those Hall of Fame Christians who has willfully chosen to rejoice through a storm and has discovered the power of perseverance, then God will trust you to handle situations and circumstances in life that He would not entrust to others.

"...and proven character, hope; and hope does not disappoint, because the love of God has been poured out within our hearts through the Holy Spirit who was given to us."
                                                          - Romans 5:3-5

We are the people of hope who serve the God of all hope. It's what we do well: we hope well! Construction workers build and teachers instruct; retailers sell and waitresses serve; Christians hope!

We don't count the number of trials or tribulations that we experience, but we count it an honor to hope in a mighty big God. Hope is anticipating the goodness of God himself to intervene in your circumstances. When you remain hopeful no matter what you are going through, you will never be disappointed because of God's love. God's love has been spilled out in abundance upon the caverns of your life so that you are able to glory in every situation. Situations no longer have the power to disappoint you but they instead bring out the very best in you. The love of God has been poured lavishly out into your heart, which is the birthplace of your emotional responses to life. When you are loved, everything else is minor. When you know that you are unconditionally loved, nothing is able to disappoint you.

God! Where are You?!

"Yet You are holy, O You who are enthroned upon the praises of Israel. In You our fathers trusted; they trusted and You delivered them. To You they cried out and were delivered; in You they trusted and were not disappointed."

- Psalm 22:3-5

If there is one place that God feels at home, it is in your praises. God sits down, puts up His lovely feet and relaxes when a believer chooses to worship. Conversely, when you throw a tantrum and rant and rave and shout out blame toward heaven, God is uncomfortable dwelling in that place. Our hearts are the dwelling places of God and we must be very careful as we determine the kind of atmosphere that we have created for the Lord to live in. I have learned in so many situations in my life, that the Lord is more interested in my heart than He is in changing my circumstances. Because the cry of my heart is to be more like Him every day, then, I, too, must have greater regard and pay more prayerful attention to what is developing in my heart than what is happening in my circumstances. We ask God to change our circumstances when what He desires is for our circumstances to change us.

As a woman of God, you have a choice to either magnify your pain and your disappointing circumstances or magnify your God in spite of your pain. Some of us talk more about our sadness and distress than we do about the Lord whom we serve. I can always tell by what a woman talks about what she has chosen, either consciously or subconsciously, to magnify.

When you place all of your trust in God, you will never be disappointed. If your trust is in your circumstances or in the people around you, you will marinate in the atmospheric conditions of disappointment. But when you focus on Jesus, you will never deal with overwhelming disappointment because there is simply no disappointment in Him. Ever.

"For the Scripture says, 'Whoever believes in Him will not be disappointed.'"

- Romans 10:11

As I meditate on the great men and women of God in the Bible who chose to serve Him and were used significantly at their historical time, there is not one who did not have to deal with disappointment. Esther was an orphan raised by a bachelor uncle and yet God used her to save the entire nation of Jews. Joseph was ridiculed by his brothers and was sold into slavery and yet he rose to second in command in Egypt and strategized to save his countrymen from severe famine. Daniel was kidnapped out of his childhood home and was forced into a den of ravenous, fierce lions and yet God used him as a force for righteousness in Babylon. What has your disappointment in life been? God is not finished with you yet and He works with

His children until He wins! Your disappointment does not have the power to dis-appoint you but may actually place you in a strategic position to be used by God.

A Broken Heart

There is, indeed, such a thing as a broken heart and the Bible poignantly and powerfully helps women of every generation deal with the issues that break our hearts. A broken heart is epically greater than mere disappointment and whips into our lives with a force that leaves everything forever changed. A broken heart will make you wretch with pain and heave with sorrow. A broken heart will leave you gasping for breath.

What has the power to break a woman's heart? The "other woman" has the power to smash a heart and leave it lying on the ground in thousands of little pieces. The rejection by one's own children or the early death of a child causes monstrous devastation to a woman's heart. Knowing that there certainly are circumstances that have the potential to leave a parade of broken hearts in their wake, how does a Christian deal with a broken heart? Is it possible for a believer to grapple with a broken heart in a different manner than non-believers? God truly does have a strategy for broken hearts that is able to put your life – and your heart – back together again. When God does the mending, the healed heart is actually healthier after the break than it was prior to the devastation.

God knew that while we are living this side of heaven that there would be people, events and issues that would break the hearts of His beloved children and so He has a plan for the most devastating moment in your life:

"The LORD is near to the brokenhearted and saves those who are crushed in spirit."

- Psalm 34:18

The word "broken" in Hebrew is the word *shabar* and it means "to rend violently, wreck or crush; to maim, cripple, to shatter or break." The ancient Hebrew is a very descriptive language and so this word *shabar* comes not only with a listed definition, but also with situations that it was used in the description of. This word was used to describe ships that had been splintered and torn from stem to stern due to ferocious and wild winds. It was also used to describe the action of tearing and ripping that wild, ravenous beasts performed upon their prey. It could literally be translated "the ruptured hearted ones."

The word for "heart" in this particular scripture is the word *leb* and it is referring to the soul or heart of a man. It encompasses one's moral character, appetites, emotions, passions and even the mind and the memory.

So, when the Psalmist declares that *"The Lord is near to the brokenhearted,"* his words are words spoken with tender care and great compassion. He is reminding all of Christendom in the epochs yet to come that the Lord is lovingly attentive to those who are enduring unimaginable pain. This pain may have been caused by a great tempest in your life or by a wild and ferocious person, but the Lord is standing attentively beside you paying diligent attention to your shattered and bleeding heart.

If you have ever suffered from this torturous condition, I can assure you that you were never out of God's care. If, today, you are emotionally torn apart and wonder how you will make it through one more today, I want to comfort you with the surety that *He is with you now.* God is close to you and has wrapped His arms of love around your life; He is hovering beside you just as a caring nurse would tend to a victim of an accident.

"You've Had a Difficult Time"

When I was pregnant with our second son, Christopher, I was induced at three weeks and two days past my due date. His birth weight was 9 pounds, 11 ounces and his delivery was extremely difficult and traumatic. I pushed for nearly four hours before the doctor decided that I would require help to deliver this very large, post-due baby. The doctor used what was known as "high forceps" and it was an agonizing physical experience after a long and arduous labor. When Christopher Burton McLeod was finally delivered on January 27, 1983, and pronounced healthy, he was whisked away to the nursery and I was wheeled down the hallway to the recovery room.

I remember lying on the cold, hard table in the darkness shaking from head to toe, trying not to whimper from the trauma. A small, Norwegian nurse came to my bedside and seemed like an angelic vision to me. She had golden braids wrapped around her head with a light blue sweater covering her white nurse's uniform. She took my cold hand in her warm one and whispered, "I've heard you've had a difficult time, dear one."

The tears were rolling down my cheeks as I weakly whispered in response, "I just want to know that my baby is ok."

"Oh, he will be just fine. They are taking excellent care of him in the nursery and I am going to take care of you here," she comforted with a thick, Scandinavian accent. With that, she encouraged me to close my eyes and rest and that she would take care of my bruised and bleeding body. She had warm clothes and towels on the cart and truly ministered in a physical way as I dealt with the aftermath of an indescribable labor. She then rubbed my arms and legs with soothing and warm oil as she sang gently over me in a language that I had never before heard.

When this Norwegian vision had thoroughly cleaned and restored my body, she brought warm broth to me and fed me spoonful by spoonful, as she cooed over me what a beautiful baby I had just delivered and how he would accomplish great things with his life. After praying a sweet, gentle prayer over me and my sweet boy, she smiled and walked away.

It was only a minute or two more before Craig was allowed to come in the recovery room and be with me. I told him all about her and could not control my sobs because of her precious care and concern toward me.

The next day, when I had been sent to the obstetrical ward, I asked my young nurse if I could send a thank you note to the woman who had cared for me in the recovery room the day before. She said that she would be glad to take it down to her on her break. I painstakingly wrote a note from my heart and thanked her deeply for her love and ministrations.

When my nurse returned to the floor after her break, she said, "Mrs. McLeod, I am sorry but no one by that description works in the recovery room. I even asked the head nurse who was assigned to the afternoon shift yesterday afternoon and she said that no one fitting that description has ever worked here." She patted my hand and regretfully handed my priceless note back to me.

I knew in that moment that I had been in the presence of an angel, unaware, hailing not from Scandinavia but from heaven. What joy to know that the Lord was close to me when I needed Him the most!

Don't Push Him Away

If you have a broken heart, or know someone who does, you can count on God's presence and His closeness to bind up your wounds and to begin the healing process. Do not push Him away at these moments of brokenness but welcome Him gladly and receive the comfort that He has for you. So many Christians squeeze God out of their lives at the very time they need Him most desperately and when He has promised to stay close. Even men and women who have served the Lord and loved Him for decades, when suffering from a broken heart, seek comfort in other things such as alcohol, overeating, shopping or bitterness. Ladies, may I gently remind you, that *no one will comfort you like the Lord.*

If your heart has been broken, please stay in church. If your life has been ravaged, continuously play worship music and allow it to draw you into God's sweet and holy presence. Invite women over to your home to pray for you and ask friends both near and far to remember you in prayer on a daily basis while you are in God's recovery room. One practical habit that I have found particularly healing is to write down all of my favorite scriptures on 3 by 5 cards as well as on sticky notes and then I place them on my bathroom mirror, on my kitchen cabinets, on the dashboard of my car and in every other strategic location where my eyes often land.

Healed By the Word

Emily, our oldest son Matthew's wife, is a health buff and an athlete. As you already know, she eats an all-organic, gluten-free, dairy-free diet. Emily and Matthew have two incredible kids and Emily ran five miles a day through both of her pregnancies. She actually ran five miles the day before she gave birth to her world-changing kids!

During the summer of 2010, Emily noticed that she was losing control of her legs and often lost feeling in her arms and hands. She was unable to hold a cup of hot tea in her hands or walk up and down the stairs. This long-distance athlete was no longer able to perform the simply daily tasks for herself or for her family. After endless medical tests and appointments with a variety of specialists, Emily, at 28 years old, was diagnosed with multiple sclerosis, commonly known as MS.

After the initial shock wore off, Emily rose to the occasion both physically and spiritually. She read everything that she could concerning the disease and traveled to distant cities to meet with nutritionists and health experts. Emily changed her diet again to combat any long-term effects of the medical diagnosis. She began going to the top neurologist in her city and began researching medical opinions on drugs and other options.

But, most importantly, Emily put on her spiritual boxing gloves and began to do lethal warfare with the enemy. She quickly made phone appointments with two medical doctors who not only believed in the God-given ability of medical knowledge but also honored the healing power of God. One of these men had, himself, been diagnosed with MS nearly 25 years ago and to date, has experienced no long term effects of the disease due to prayer and a healthy diet.

The other doctor who has guided Emily through her battle is one of the most well respected internists in the country. Duke Medical Center, the Mayo Clinic and Johns Hopkins all call this esteemed physician for second opinions. When 9-11 occurred, this doctor was flown into seclusion with the Supreme Court Justices in case of a national attack. This doctor is a man of God who is tearing down serious medical strongholds through the power of prayer. Every single person on his staff is taught to pray for each patient every day. This man, who makes the enemy curl up in a fetal position, put Emily on a spiritual regimen of prayer and the Word of God.

When you enter Emily's home, the Word is everywhere. It is on her bathroom mirror and on her computer screen. She has plaques with scriptures on her walls and piles of devotional books on her bedside table. Scriptures are on the dashboard of her car and worship music is played while her children sleep.

When your heart is broken and the peace of God is a distant and tenuous fog, allow the Word of God to dwell in you richly! The

Word of God has healing power not only for your physical body but also for your broken heart.

"He sent His word and healed them, and delivered them from their destructions."

- Psalm 107:20

Counterfeit Healing

The enemy often attempts to imitate God and to falsely produce a counterfeit answer to our problems that will ultimately end in destruction. If you have a broken heart, the enemy will first of all entice you to play the blame game. You will blame others, yourself and finally, you will blame God for your broken heart. Do not play the blame game with the enemy! We are not a people who blame God but we are a people who bless God. So, if your heart has been broken and you are tempted to begin to throw blame, instead shout to the heavens, "I will not blame but I will bless the Lord!"

The enemy will try to keep you out of church, away from fellowship, off your knees and disinterested in the Word of God. The enemy will whisper lies into your broken heart to try to convince you that other things hold more healing power than God does: *"You don't need to go to church. You need to stay home and just enjoy a quiet morning with a cup of coffee. You just need to think about everything you have been through. You will feel better after you clean your house."*

Ladies! Attention! If there is anyplace that you truly need to be when you are trying to heal from a broken heart it is in the House of God with the people of God! Miracles happen in church and God's Word is exalted in church. People will pray for you at church and you will be in the presence of worship! Go to church, brokenhearted and all!

"Reading the Bible really isn't going to help you today. It's so hard to understand and the words are just not sinking in because your heart is broken. You don't have the attention span to read the Word right now. God understands."

God does not understand why His children would rebuff the greatest Love Letter of all time. The Bible was not primarily written for information but for transformation. If you desire your broken heart to be transformed into pure gold, then you will read the Word, even when you don't "get it" with your mind. The Bible is a not a flat book but it is a dynamic experience and creates miracles at the worst moments of our lives!

The devil is a diabolical, twisted entity who endeavors to kick the people of God when they are down. Kick him back! Snuggle into the closeness of God when your heart has been broken by the stuff of life and He will protect you from the devil and his schemes. It is in the presence of God where the devil is not able to reach you mentally or emotionally.

I Object!

There is a well-treasured saying that even Christians take comfort from during times of duress and tragedy, *"Time heals all wounds."*

May I just tell you loudly…I OBJECT!! Time has no inherent healing power. Only God has healing power! I know women who are just as bitter and angry today as they were ten years ago. Time hasn't healed their souls. I know women who are playing the blame game louder today than they were 30 years ago. Time has not healed these exhausted, hoarse women.

Only Jesus has healing power and so if you have a broken heart and long for comfort, then you must burrow into His presence where miracles happen not because of time, but because of Him. Are you allowing the nurturing closeness that He gives especially to the brokenhearted to heal your heart today?

How Do You Mend a Broken Heart?

"He heals the brokenhearted and binds up their wounds."

- Psalm 147:3

No one can mend a broken heart but the Lord. Other people's words will encourage you and bring a measure of healing but the ultimate healing is always from the Lord. Kind deeds and gestures may remove the sting from a broken heart, but nothing and no one other than the Lord can place that crowning healing touch on your life. He has the power, love and divine skill to actually cure you from the extraordinary pain that you are going through.

God is able to restore your soul and perform a spiritual heart transplant if that is what it takes to move you into health and hope again. This seems impossible when you have a broken heart but it is not impossible to God! The will of God is always restoration and healing.

We can easily understand the concept that the Holy Spirit is endeavoring to communicate through the psalmist in the phrase, *"...and binds up their wounds."* The word picture that is being painted through the Hebrew language is the beautiful illustration of a tailor gently mending and sewing together that which was torn apart. If you have a broken heart, friend, I know Someone who has the expert skills to easily and perfectly mend it. Not only is He able to repair your broken heart, but He has the desire to do it.

The Great Exchange

I know a woman who runs the farm that has been in her family for generations. She loves what she does and has not only a house filled with domestic pets, but also a yard filled with outdoor pets and a barn filled with 4-legged creatures. Each animal, regardless of the species, has a name and is known by their quirks and preferences. When you walk into her formal living room, on the mantle are beautiful vases and containers of different shapes, sizes and colors. She will tearfully give you a tour of her mantle and tell you which pet's ashes are in each container and what each animal meant to her.

Animal lovers of the world…please don't get upset with me. I like pets. We used to have a parade of dogs through our children's growing up years. These canine darlings lived in my home and in my heart. I cried…sobbed really…when each pet died. But I did not preserve their ashes and put them on display for the entire world to see and remember.

What ashes do you have hanging around your life? Could it possibly be time to exchange your ashes for something of far greater value?

"The Spirit of the Lord GOD is upon me, because the LORD has anointed me to bring good news to the afflicted; He has sent me to bind up the brokenhearted, to proclaim liberty to captives and freedom to prisoners; to proclaim the favorable year of the LORD and the day of vengeance of our God; to comfort all who mourn, to grant those who mourn in Zion, giving them a garland instead of ashes, the oil of gladness instead of mourning, the mantle of praise instead of a spirit of fainting. So they will be called oaks of righteousness, the planting of the LORD, that He may be glorified."

- Isaiah 61:1-3

Most Christians are familiar with the classic beauty of this scripture found deep in the heart of Isaiah, the great prophet of the Old Testament. Likewise, most Christians know that Jesus himself quoted these verses when He returned to His hometown of Nazareth and was asked to read the Scriptures one Sabbath Day. But most of us are not making the great exchange that Jesus called us to in these spectacular verses with a miraculous promise.

The plan of God was that He would send Jesus to do the greatest exchange in all of recorded history. We would give Him our sin and He would give us His righteousness. We would give Him our sickness and He would give to us His healing power. We would give to Him our ashes and He would exchange them for a beautiful garland. We would give to Him all of the things that make us sad, and He would give us in return the oil of gladness. What a deal! What have you to lose? Why do you still have your ashes and your brokenness hanging around your life when you could partner with Christ in the great exchange?!

The purpose of the Cross is far-reaching and certainly not singular in purpose. Jesus died for our sins so that we could live a life of forgiveness on earth and then spend all of eternity in His presence. We also know that the Scriptures declare that we were healed because of the stripes that Jesus suffered upon His back. But do not ever discount the fact that Jesus died for your emotional health as well.

"Surely our griefs He Himself bore, and our sorrows He carried."

- Isaiah 53:4

Jesus has taken all of the things that have broken your heart to the cross of Calvary. He personally carried each disappointment and anything that caused you emotional pain. He took the events that brought emotional pain into your heart and He died for those things on the old rugged cross. He did it because He wanted you to live an abundant life on earth! He did not want you to carry the grief and the sorrow and so He did it for you. He did it in your place. He took it so that you could carry the joy and gladness and rejoicing with you throughout your entire life. You don't have to carry the pain...it has already been carried and has been laid at the foot of the cross.

In the Valley of the Shadow

"Even though I walk through the valley of the shadow of death, I fear no evil, for You are with me; Your rod and Your staff, they comfort me. You prepare a table before me in the presence of my enemies; You have anointed my head with oil; my cup overflows. Surely goodness and lovingkindness will follow me all the days of my life, and I will dwell in the house of the LORD forever."

- Psalm 23:4-6

Finally, allow me to gently and tenderly remind you that God has not stopped being God because you are in the valley. He has not stopped being a God of goodness and kindness because you are either disappointed or have a broken heart.

We would all love to spend our lives on the top of a mountain. We would all love to vigorously breathe in that fresh mountain air and take in the magnificent view. You can see things on the mountaintop that you would never see from the valley. Things take on their rightful perspective from the mountaintop. You are literally on top of the world. It's a place fit for a queen...the queen of the mountain!

None of us wants to buy real estate in the valley of despair and disappointment. There is an extremely limited vision in the lower places and you are not able to see beyond the next grove of trees.

And yet it is in the valley where vegetation grows and where flowers bloom. There is no growth on the top of a mountain but you will only find rocks and boulders there. The top of a mountain is no place to put down roots...that happens in the valley below. It is in the valley where the most magnificent growth of your life will happen and it is there that the fruit of the Spirit will grow in lush abundance. May I just say it this way: The valley where your heart was broken will be the place of your greatest harvest.

God wants our cups to run over not only when life is good and the view is spectacular; He wants our cups to run over in the valley of pain and in the desert of brokenness. God sets before you a table of blessing that will heal your broken heart and feed your hungry soul.

God wants you to be a woman who knows that disappointment does not have the power to dis-appoint her. God wants you to be a woman who snuggles into His presence during times of brokenness and despair. God wants you to be a woman who never blames but always blesses. God wants you to be a woman who bears fruit at the worst moment of her life.

Are you that woman?

(11)

What Will Your Legacy Be?

If you only read one chapter in this entire book, this is the chapter that you *must* read. This will not be an easy chapter to read, but it is the one that has the most potential to give you the tools that you need to live your life as an emotionally healthy woman. This chapter is sobering, yet will enable you to realize the consequences that Christians have to face when they allow themselves to be consumed with self rather than with Christ. Your life will only be a caricature of the person that the Lord intended to reveal through your life if you remain obstinate in your demands to have it your way and not His way. If you stubbornly refuse to exhibit humility, gentleness and peacefulness and continue to be a woman of selfish ambition, jealousy and arrogance, then you will never become the masterpiece that God created you to be. God created you for majestic living and for revealing His glory even through your emotional habits! Do not settle for less than the abundance that Jesus came to give you today.

The Battle for Your Emotions

We do, indeed, have an enemy who is in constant warfare with us because he does not want us to live the life that God has in store for all of us.

"The thief comes only to steal and kill and destroy; I came that they may have life, and have it abundantly."

- John 10:10

The devil has one intention and that is to rob you of your abundant life and he is relentless in his attempts to do so. Many of the weapons in the enemy's arsenal are emotional reactions because he cannot touch our spirits and so his twisted plan is to communicate with our soul. The enemy will try to deceive any one of us into thinking that we deserve to walk in unforgiveness or that no one understands our particular pain. When we agree with him in his deception, our emotional habits will mimic the devil's choices rather than God's abundance. Now that's scary!

One of the most obvious ways that Satan tries to deny Christians their ability to live an abundant life is by trying to convince them that they are entitled to negative emotions. The devil is thrilled when you agree with him that you are indeed entitled to worry, exhibit unforgiveness or show outrageous anger and then he rubs his nasty little hands together with glee when he tricks you into blatantly throwing a hissy fit of human ugliness. God does not want you to agree with the devil: He wants you to be like Him. God loves you enough to discipline you until you concede that neither you nor the devil has a better idea than God!

"All discipline for the moment seems not to be joyful, but sorrowful; yet to those who have been trained by it, afterwards it yields the peaceful fruit of righteousness. Therefore, strengthen the hands that are weak and the knees that are feeble, and make straight paths for your feet, so that the limb which is lame may not be put out of joint, but rather be healed."

- Hebrews 12:11–13

Whether you are 8 or 88, no one enjoys the process of discipline. I don't like to be disciplined and I never truly enjoyed disciplining my own children, although I knew that it was necessary for their potential to mature into well-adjusted, contributing members not only of society but also of the Kingdom of God. Anyone who desires to be used in a consequential way by God, understands the divine prerequisite in overcoming one's own fleshly responses to life. Your flesh, which also can be recognized as your human emotions, stands in opposition to your spirit and to God's Spirit in you, unless you have learned not only to discipline the flesh but crucify it as well.

If your most passionate desire is to be a grand display of the fruit of the Spirit and the personality of God, the price that you must pay is to crucify the flesh and to discipline your emotions. If you are able to cooperate with God in this difficult endeavor, you will be positioning yourself for availability in carrying out God's significant plan at this time in history.

People Watching

One of my favorite pastimes in life is to "people watch." When my children were young, we played a private, family game whenever we were out in public. We would try to guess people's occupations by how they dressed, their manner of walking or speaking and by their facial expressions. If we were in the airport, we would sit – all seven

McLeod's – in one row watching the passengers walk by our row of outfacing seats.

If a scholarly, well-dressed gentleman walked by, you could hear someone whisper, "College professor."

"Professional tennis player," was the quiet input while observing a buff, 20-something, tanned specimen walk down the airport corridor.

And when a large woman with a frizzy perm and out of date glasses passed us carrying her black leather purse with two books tucked under her arm, we would all say in unison, "Librarian!"

As the mother of five children, each delivered with individual personalities and preferences, I must say that when my firstborn was only a couple of months old, I began to observe mothers. I longed to do mothering well and had no experience on which to base my style. When Matthew was only a few months old, whether I was in the park, at the mall or in church, I became a passionate observer of mothers. And, if I saw a mother doing a particularly outstanding job with her children, I would shyly approach her, introduce myself and begin to interview her relentlessly!

Over the years, as I gained more experience, I began to watch young mothers with a more critical eye rather than an experimental one. The approach to parenting that troubles me the most happens when mothers allow their children to do whatever their little heart desires with no parental guidance or discipline. Children need caring, wise adults in their lives in order to guide them into maturity. Children are, by their very nature, only immature, undisciplined models of adults and will never grow into the best versions of themselves without training and discipline.

When you look at a child with no true parental discipline or training, you have obtained a front seat view of what happens when the flesh is left to its own pleasure. A child, left on his or her own, will most likely sleep all day and stay up all night; this free youthful spirit will eat chips and brownies and never touch food items like broccoli and green beans. A young person who is left to make his or her own choices without parental boundaries will watch inappropriate television programs, use vulgar language and waste hundreds of waking hours playing video or computer games.

I have also just painted a picture of a Christian who goes through life ruled by the flesh rather than by the Spirit of God, which is inside each one of us. Dealing with our flesh and our fleshly desires is certainly like disciplining an out of control child. This process of discipline, or chastening, can be so painful but the rewards are heavenly!

It Hurts!

"All discipline, for the moment seems not to be joyful, but sorrowful ..."
- Hebrews 12:11

The word for "discipline" that the Holy Spirit used in this verse in Hebrews, comes from an old Greek word that referred to the education or instruction of a child. Through the years, this word evolved until during the time of Plato, this word now encompassed not only the training of a child but also the training of adults. In other verses in the New Testament, this same Greek word, which is *paideia* is translated as "chastise" and is used when describing the scene when Jesus was brutally whipped as punishment.

Whenever it is necessary for the Holy Spirit to deal with our outrageous emotional responses to life, it will not be initially joyful but it will be painful. The word "discipline" in this verse from Hebrews refers to disciplinary attitudes and actions that lead to one's betterment in life. The fact that this word can also refer to painful punishment clearly communicates to us, who endeavor to serve Christ in the 21st Century, that often pain is required so that fruit can be produced in our lives.

It is not easy dying to self and it is even more difficult choosing not to say what is on our minds, but we must discipline ourselves to only respond to difficult people and challenging situations with the fruit of the Holy Spirit. Pain is a part of the process of sanctifying your emotional sludge and the sooner that you restrain yourself, the less pain you will encounter.

I hate doing laundry and cleaning our bathrooms…but I do it because it betters the life of my family. I find no intrinsic joy in mopping the kitchen floor or changing the sheets on our beds…but I do it because it is a benefit to the people whom I love the most.

I am not interested in math or science and have struggled through many, many high school and college courses taught by brilliant and competent teachers who were unable to make sense of those confusing and utterly unexplainable courses to my vacuous mind. But, I studied physics, calculus and geometry in high school because I wanted to do well on the SAT and thereby be awarded college scholarships. You, too, should make yourself learn difficult emotional lessons in order to pass the tests of life and earn the blessings that God has for you when you choose to embrace His nature and deny yourself!

I make my post-menopausal body jog on nearly a daily basis so that I am able to control my weight and be as healthy as possible as I grow older. But marathon runners jog differently than my pitiful attempt at completing two miles in just under 30 painful minutes. Runners who are preparing for long distance races habitually run 10-15 miles a day up and down hills and with weights on their muscular legs. They do it so they can win…so they can finish strong and be awarded the medal that goes only to the first few finishers.

The goal of your emotional marathon is to be a fruit-bearing Christian; it is not to demand your own way, tell your side of the story or defend your out-of-control actions. The disciplinary process that you are going to face while you train your flesh to die is not joyful but sorrowful and painful. Some of you may feel like crying as you read this chapter because it takes discipline to get the self out of us and the Christ into us.

The benefits of any type of discipline are numerous and life-changing, but the process of disciplining our emotions causes our flesh to have a disgusting knee-jerk reaction as it cries out in pain at the perceived injustice.

"Why don't I get to express myself? Everyone else does!"

"But it wasn't my fault and she is blaming me for it! Why can't I tell my side of the story and defend myself?!"

"But he never remembers my birthday and I am sick of it!"

"My mother is always on my case…always critiquing and complaining.

I am a grown woman and I can do it my own way for once!"

The flesh hates to be disciplined and so it cries and wails and complains. However, your flesh must die a full and complete death so that your spirit and your emotions can be alive to God. When your spirit and your emotions have settled this issue, you will be a luscious, fruit-bearing Christian who is providing sustenance and delight to a famine-filled world.

The Bible says that this process of discipline has yet another cause and effect, "…*yet to those who have been trained by it, afterwards it yields the peaceful fruit of righteous.*"

The word "trained" in this phrase is a powerful word that is not intended for the faint of heart but only for those who are willing to sweat and ache and go the entire distance. It is the Greek word, *gumnadzo* and it is actually a picture of radical discipline. It is the same word used in Ancient Greece to describe the athletes who were preparing for Olympic competition and chose to exercise and train arduously. This word conveys the image of a select group of competitors who are so passionate about developing into their fullest potential that they are willing to put themselves through the most strenuous and perhaps even torturous exercises in order to be called a champion!

If you can see the value in schooling your flesh and your emotions, you are going to achieve great results. Most of us want the results without the process. We want the promise without the pain. We long for the reward without the re-conditioning. We want the fruit of the Spirit while still hacking up the phlegm of the flesh. You cannot have both. You can either have the fruit or the flesh. You can either have the fruit or the feelings. You choose.

If your heart's desire is to yield the peaceful fruit of righteousness then you will be required to teach your flesh some lessons that it has been unwilling to learn. If you keep doing the same thing in the same way, you will always get the same results. But if you want different results, you must do different things in a different way. If you can see the value in producing a bumper crop of peace and righteousness in your life, you will be required to do something more than you have been doing. You will be required to say no to the flesh and to selfishness. You will place healthy boundaries around your emotions and realize that your feelings do not always tell the truth.

My Internal Civil War

When you are writing a book, all of the experts and editors agree: don't have long passages of Scripture in the book. Truthfully, that advice is like fingernails on the chalkboard of life to somebody like me! I am a Bible teacher...it is what I do...I quote the Word of God and extract practical principles from the wisdom found only in the Bible. I just believe that if it is not already said in the Word, then I probably shouldn't say it. I solidly affirm that the Holy Spirit is so much more creative and intuitive than I am so let's start with the Word and then ask for practical application. Do you agree with me? I was hoping that you would because I am about to quote a l-o-n-g passage of Scripture that you need to read! It's going to be good for you and after reading this passage, you are going to understand yourself emotionally so much better. I promise. I really do.

Let's listen in to a conversation that Paul is having with the Christians in Rome. Paul is confessing to them how hard it is for him to obey God and although he longs to do it, he is just so divided. I believe that as you read these words, penned nearly 2,000 years ago, that you will see yourself and relate to Paul's battle. This passage of Scripture is quoted from *The Message Bible* which is a paraphrase and not a word for word translation. But I believe as you read these verses written in today's vernacular, you will clearly understand the heart of Paul and perhaps your own heart.

"I know that all God's commands are spiritual, but I'm not. Isn't this also your experience?" Yes. I'm full of myself – after all, I've spent a long time in sin's prison. What I don't understand about myself is that I decide one way, but then I act another, doing things I abso-

lutely despise. So if I can't be trusted to figure out what is best for myself and then do it, it becomes obvious that God's command is necessary.

But I need something more! For if I know the law but still can't keep it, and if the power of sin within me keeps sabotaging my best intentions, I obviously need help! I realize that I don't have what it takes. I can will it, but I can't do it. I decide to do good, but I don't really do it; I decide not to do bad, but then I do it anyway. My decisions, such as they are, don't result in actions. Something has gone wrong deep within me and gets the better of me every time.

It happens so regularly that it's predictable. The moment I decide to do good, sin is there to trip me up. I truly delight in God's commands, but it's pretty obvious that not all of me joins in that delight. Parts of me covertly rebel, and just when I least expect it, they take charge.

I've tried everything and nothing helps. I'm at the end of my rope. Is there no one who can do anything for me? Isn't that the real question?

The answer, thank God, is that Jesus Christ can and does. He acted to set things right in this life of contradictions where I want to serve God with all my heart and mind, but am pulled by the influence of sin to do something totally different.

- Romans 7:14-25

Don't you see yourself emotionally in these verses? Paul has experienced exactly what you go through on a daily basis! You don't want to give your husband the silent treatment...but you do! You don't want to yell at your kids...but you do! You don't want to be mean to your mother...but you are! You don't want to gossip or think mean thoughts or have a critical spirit...but you do all those things and more!

What you really want is to be like Jesus...and yet the struggle continues...

You Are the Target

I believe that Satan goes after Christians more directly and passionately than he does after the unsaved. He has so much more to lose at our hands. There is nothing that scares Satan more than a powerful Christian who is filled with the Holy Spirit and is exhibiting the fruit of this relationship. Satan knows that when Christians die to the flesh and are filled with and guided by the Holy Spirit, that we become a vast and mighty army destined for victory in every area of our lives. As a result, Satan attacks Christians because he knows that when we tap into the power of God, he will never again stand a chance.

There are some emotions that open us up to spiritual warfare in a way that others do not. You can have a moment of anger without becoming an angry person. However, if you do not handle your moment of anger righteously but allow the anger to sit and simmer and grow, then you will indeed become an angry person and you will have opened yourself up to a spirit of anger. A spirit of anger will torment you daily and attempt to enter all of your conversations. A spirit of anger will endeavor to warp all of your relationships and steal your abundant life. This does not mean that you are demon-possessed, it just means that the spirit of anger knows your address and will be continually knocking at the door of your heart until you deal with the anger in the manner that the Word of God instructs you to deal with it.

"Pursue peace with all men, and the sanctification without which no one will see the Lord. See to it that no one comes short of the grace of God; that no root of bitterness springing up causes trouble, and by it many be deviled."

- Hebrews 12:14-15

You can choose not to forgive once without becoming a bitter person, but if you refuse to forgive time after time after time, un-forgiveness will open the door of your heart to have a conversation with a spirit of bitterness. This does not mean that you are demon-possessed, it just means that your heart is entertaining a spirit of bitterness. Bitterness has a way of putting its foot in the door of your heart and forcing entry into your life. It has a way of making itself at home in your life and putting its roots down deep and rapidly. Bitterness is a fast growing, crawling emotion that will weave in and out of the healthy places in your life until every area of your life has been infected. A spirit of bitterness will torment you daily and never leave you alone. Bitterness will petrify all of your friendship and will paralyze your ability to walk toward your destiny. Bitterness has the evil power to contaminate your family with this generational curse and disease for generations to come.

"But one whom you forgive anything, I forgive also; for indeed what I have forgiven, if I have forgiven anything, I did it for your sakes in the presence of Christ, so that no advantage would be taken of us by Satan, for we are not ignorant of his schemes."

- II Corinthians 2:10 & 11

We are called to forgive those who have wronged us in order to keep Satan from having an advantage over us. When we forgive others, not only is it advantageous for them, but it is especially advantageous for us because unforgiveness in our lives will open the door for spiritual warfare that is totally unnecessary. Some spiritual warfare is necessary; all of us have to face it and fight it. However, some of the battles that we face in the spiritual realm are a result of our unforgiveness, our daily problem with anger, or a root of bitterness that we have allowed to grow unrestricted in our lives. The devil would love to keep you involved in warfare every day of your life so that you can never move ahead in victory. The devil is so devious that he wants to keep you fighting the same battles over and over and over again so that you are not involved in ministry or in evangelism.

The Litmus Test

Believe it or not, the Scripture says that your daily behavior and how you respond to other people are two of the litmus tests that will test your maturity or your wisdom.

"Who among you is wise and understanding? Let him show by his good behavior his deeds in the gentleness of wisdom."
- James 3:13

If you are able to control your tongue, you are growing up in Christ! If you are able to speak words of kindness when others are being cruel or impatient, that is a sign of maturity or wisdom. Wisdom is also demonstrated if, when there is a difference of opinion, you are able to humbly submit and recognize that the opinions of others may be as valid as your own. If you are controlled by your flesh, it is nearly impossible to put your hand over your mouth and choose not to spout your self-righteous point of view. But, if you are controlled by the Holy Spirit within you, it is not only possible to control your tongue but it is even probable!

If you insist on regurgitating your opinions and demonstrating a defensive attitude toward people who think differently than you think, you are being controlled by your flesh and will always be regarded as immature and foolish. Women who relentlessly demand their own way and then accuse others of not understanding are measured as foolish and immature according to the Word of God.

It is when you are under stress that these issues are most glaring and are easily measured. Anyone can be happy and sweet when she gets her own way and everyone is agreeing with her opinions. A woman is a delightful wife, mother and friend when the bills are paid, the kids are behaving and the husband has taken out the trash. However, only a mature woman of God is able to respond with grace and patience while under pressure. This verse from James tells us that when we behave with wisdom, we are always gentle. Are you gentle? Wisdom will never exhibit a crude or unkind approach to a situation.

"But if you have bitter jealousy and selfish ambition in your heart, do not be arrogant and so lie against the truth. This wisdom is not that which comes down from above, but is earthly, natural and demonic. For where jealousy and selfish ambition exist, there is disorder and every evil thing."

- James 3:14-16

If you have an intense ambition to advance your opinions or ideas to the near exclusion of others' opinions and ideas, you are in jeopardy of ushering in a spirit of strife. The devil loves it when we are full of ourselves, refuse to listen to others and insist on doing all of the talking. He knows at that point, that he can use the opinionated, argumentative Christian to actually cause division. Satan loves to instigate civil wars and it is always his tactic to goad a Christian, through a spirit of pride, to fire the first shot.

If you are always promoting yourself, you are in very dangerous territory because there is nothing of heaven in this heart attitude. James says that arrogance, which includes self-promotion and domineering conversations, in no way reflects the nature of heaven and of Christ. It is an earthly way to handle a situation, not a heavenly way. James also describes this heart attitude as "soulish" which means that it was not birthed in your spirit man but in your soul. Then, James continues to describe an opinionated, selfish person, as not only earthly and soulish but also as devilish. The Greek word that is used in this phrase is *daimoniodes* and is best translated as "demonized" which paints the picture of a person whose mind or emotions (soul) have come under the influence of demon spirits. Now that scares me! I do not want to be that woman, do you? I do not want to be so filled with self-promotion and prideful opinions that I give the devil a foothold in my life. Some of us need to get down on our knees right now and ask God to forgive us for being so opinionated about things that really don't matter.

I have political opinions. I have strong, valid, well thought out political opinions. I am actually what some people would call "politically savvy." My opinions are birthed out of being well read, comparing political opinions to the Word of God, and doing my homework when it comes to political platforms. However, not everyone in my family agrees with my opinions. Not everyone in my church agrees with my opinions. And so, I put my hand over my mouth because I do not want to cause division among the people whom I love the most. I am called, not to run for office, but I am called to bring a word of grace like *"apples of gold in settings of silver"* (Proverbs 25:11). I have had to realize that the call of God on my life should bring unity and not division and so I leave my political leanings at home. This is difficult for me because I love to talk politics and interview others concerning their political bent and opinions. But rather than cause strife, I painfully choose to stay quiet about a subject that would potentially divide and not promote unity.

When you allow jealousy and selfish ambition to make a home in your heart, you *think* that you are wise and you think that you know best but actually, what is happening is that your flesh is being cheered on by the demonic. The world in which we live magnifies our right to be jealous and to promote ourselves, but the world's way has never been the Word's way. The world will tell you that you are entitled to think thoughts like these:

"I am better than you are...I am prettier and smarter and skinnier."

"I want to be better than you are. I don't like you because you are prettier and smarter and skinnier than I am."

"Why can she have it all and I can't?! I deserve it, too!"

If you have a tendency to think in those particular thought patterns, it is bitter jealousy and the Bible calls it demonic. When we give in to our cultural, fleshly reactions to life, we are opening the door to the devil. That is one guest who should never be welcome in your life!

"For where jealousy and selfish ambition exist, there is disorder and every evil thing."

- James 3:16

If you do not rid yourself of jealousy and selfish ambition, disorder and other evil traits will enter your life. You will be inundated with devilish thinking and demonic attitudes when you entertain the green-eyed monster, who we now know to be not a monster at all but a demon. Jealousy opens the door to a life filled with disorder, confusion and rebellion. James actually says that "every evil thing" will become a part of your life simply because you chose to be a selfish woman. Simply stated, only bad things are birthed from your self-promoting attempts in life. If you are jealous, bad things will follow. If you are selfish, dreadful things are on their way. If you are envious, you better run for cover because you have just invited the enemy into your life.

Envy and strife are able to destroy relationships and create dissension in life-long friendships. The devil knows that if he can fan the flame of envy and strife in your heart, that he will ruin the relationships that God intended to be a blessing to you. The devil targets friendships, family relationships, church unity and even the place where you work with these two devastating attitudes. The devil loves to incite a good fight and self-righteous opinions to create fractious behavior. Have you and your relationships been targeted by Satan? Have you allowed envy and strife to become such a part of your emotional make-up that you have caused great damage to others?

Conversely, if you are humble and are more concerned about others than you are yourself, good things will follow you around. We really have it all wrong, don't we? We think that we must promote ourselves and jockey for some important position but those heart attitudes only give birth to the uglies. When you demand your own way, in actuality, you are shooting yourself in that infamous foot that is probably in your mouth, anyway.

When you can say, "Self, sit down and shut up!" that is when good things are going to begin to happen in your life. If you are wise enough to say, "Self, you will submit even if you don't like it!" you can be sure that all of the heavenly host is going to come to your rescue and make a way where there seems to be no way. If you are mature enough to declare, "Self, you will be gracious and humble every day in every situation!" you have just captured God's attention and the blessing is on its promised way!

Our two oldest boys, Matthew and Christopher, are two years apart almost to the day. Being boys, and being close in age, all of life became a friendly, sibling competition to them. They kept charts about who won the most Nintendo battles and who scored the most points that week on the basketball court in our driveway. They would argue about who had read the most books or had eaten more vegetables on any given day. They kept a running tally of who could burp the loudest, run the fastest and say the most Bible verses from memory. These little boy competitions could quickly escalate into World War II without maternal intervention and I would quote them this Bible verse, saying, "Matt and Chris... where jealousy and selfish ambition exist, there is disorder and every evil thing! I will not allow your behavior to open up the door for disorder in my home!"

A Powerful Legacy

One of my greatest goals in teaching the Word of God to women is to be practical. Down to earth, non-pretentious and practical. I want to make the Bible come alive in everyday life situations and for you to have an "a-ha!" moment when you catch the truth of a certain passage in the Word. The verse that we are about to study is so applicable to every woman's life. Quite frankly, you will never live a life of victory and joy if you are not able to apply this vital verse to your life:

"But the wisdom from above is first pure, then peaceable, gentle, reasonable, full of mercy and good fruits, unwavering, without hypoc-

risy. And the seed whose fruit is righteousness is sown in peace by those who make peace."

- James 3:17-18

This is a spiritual grocery list that clearly states what you need in your life if you want to be known as a wise woman. This is an inventory, revealed in order from the most important ingredient all the way to the most minute component of this godly recipe for excellent moral character. James says that the most important element in a wise woman's life is purity.

Wisdom is always primarily characterized by its total lack of pretense. Wise women know beyond a shadow of a doubt that life has never been about them, is currently not about them, and will never be about them. The word "pure" can be translated as pure from every fault, immaculate. The purification process always involves heat or a burning away. If your heart's desire is to be a woman whose life exhibits the wisdom of heaven, you will experience a fire or two along your life's pathway. The fire will serve to burn away those remnants of self that remain and will reveal in a greater dimension the glory of God in your life.

Another definition of the word "pure" is "exciting reference." If purity is an intrinsic part of who you are, you are thrilled to honor God in your everyday life. Your speech habits reflect this purity, the way you dress is a demonstration of purity and your daily choices in life are "squeaky clean." A pure woman reveals not one percent of self, opinion, promotion or performance but her entire life is a glorious symphony that brings honor to the King of kings.

Anita was a woman who was working on the "purity" aspect of her life but just wasn't quite there yet. Anita had a beautiful singing voice and had to often bat away pride and self-gratification concerning her talent. One Sunday at church, she had sung a particularly beautiful song and was basking in her successful performance. Anita wasn't bragging out loud but in her heart, she knew that she had brought the house down!

After service, many people gathered around her exclaiming over her voice, the song and the atmosphere that she had helped to create. In the most unassuming voice that she could conjure up, Anita responded humbly, "Well, it was just Jesus."

Anita's mother walked by and overheard her pitiful attempt at humility, She dryly responded, "Well, it wasn't that good!"

The second ingredient in a wise woman's life is that she is peaceable. If you are really done with selfish ambition and jealousy, then your life will make peace. There is a difference between being a *peacemaker* and being a *peace-keeper*. A peace-keeper is a woman who simply waves the white flag of surrender and chooses never to stand up for anything noble or righteous. Peacemakers are willing to fight for righteousness no matter what the personal cost may be. God calls us to be peacemakers, not merely peace-keepers. Peace is only a possibility when God's ways are lifted high and promoted. We must be willing to lay down our personal agendas and hold high the non-compromising standard of the Word of God. This is a vital component of a wise woman.

The third heart attitude which wise women must embrace is that of being gentle and reasonable. When the words that I use are harsh, I am retreating back toward being a woman filled with selfish ambition and jealousy. When I immaturely use a screechy or severe tone of voice, it is a serious reminder that I still have self left in me. But, when I am responding with mature, godly wisdom I will always be gentle in my dealings with people.

The Bible tells us two things that are precious in the sight of God; the first is the death of His godly ones. (Psalm 116:15.) The other thing that is precious in God's sight is a *"gentle and quiet spirit."*

My words must be gentle, my tone of voice and actions must be gentle and even beyond outward actions, my spirit must also be gentle. Gentleness is an inside job first and then it will always reveal itself on the outside. It is not good enough to be sweet on the outside and yet be reeling with anger and jealousy on the inside. The Holy Spirit says that wise women are gentle from the inside out.

The next ingredient in a wise woman's life is that she should be *"full of mercy and good fruits."* A woman who has chosen to model the character and mindset of God while living life this side of heaven is a woman who is quick to forgive and always ready to respond with kindness, patience, gentleness and goodness. This godly woman has an emotional pantry filled with the fruit of the Holy Spirit and it is her delight to share this fruit with people in need. She always offers this service with a smile on her lips and with sheer joy in her soul. This woman is so filled to overflowing with mercy and kindness that there is not room for any selfish motives in her life. It is not 99% mercy and 1% self, but it is 100% genuine godliness that oozes out of every pore of her wise body.

The next element in her life is that she has found the courage and strength to be unwavering and undivided. This woman has one sole purpose in life: to honor God with every thought that she allows to simmer in her brain, with every word that comes out of her mouth, with every breath that she is allowed to breathe and in every minute of every day. She has found purpose and destiny in magnifying the Lord and minimizing self. Her heart motive is to live her life according to the principles found in the Word of God.

This woman is not a hypocrite but she is the "real deal." She is genuinely mature without one ounce of self left. She has not one opinion of any importance except those that agree with the Word of God. Her one heartfelt goal is to serve Christ and Him alone. She prays bold prayers and serves selflessly.

This woman is peacefully sowing seeds of righteousness every day in every garden which God allows her to attend. This woman will surely be remembered...not for her opinions or for her anger. Not for her selfish ambition or for her ability to divide relationships. Her legacy will be one of peace and righteousness. She is leaving a treasure to the generations to come that is worth more than millions of dollars in the bank. She is generously giving the most blessed endowment of all: emotional stability and spiritual maturity.

What will your legacy be?

12

Every Woman's Battle

If sex is every man's battle, then I believe that issues of the heart and emotions are every woman's battle. The astounding news is that when you tap into the wisdom of the Word of God and the power of the Holy Spirit, you are guaranteed to win whatever battle you might be facing. No longer are you a victim of vicious emotional outrage and sludge but you are more than a conqueror because of Christ's great love for you.

God really does have a plan for your daily life and His plan is one of joy, peace and victory. God desperately needs you to conquer your emotional issues because you are an important part of His grander plan at this historical juncture. If you continue to wallow in the blahs, in anger and in depression, the world will be missing out on the gift that you have been created to be. You must never think that you are just a number to God and can get away with flaunting your disappointment and fear in a disproportionate demonstration. You are not merely one of the mass of humanity, but you are a valuable resource who is able to bring significant change at this historic moment.

Will you purpose to be the best you possible? Or will you be a warped woman who deviates emotionally from the plan of God for her life? God needs you! He needs you to be a living demonstration of joy and peace when your world is falling apart. He needs you to be a beautiful masterpiece of righteousness and patience in a culture gone wild. God needs women in every generation who will declare, "My life is not about me and my feelings. My life is about serving God and revealing His character to my world!"

Esther Ahn Kim

Esther Ahn Kim was a young woman who lived an ordinary life and although she was born nearly a century ago and lived half a world away, she really is not so different from any of us. She was raised by an angry father and a loving mother. She had dreams of being a music teacher to young students and perhaps eventually falling in love and being married. She often thought of how she would raise her children differently than her parents did.

Esther was born in Korea in the early 20th Century when there was a radical political struggle occurring between Korea, China, Japan and Russia. So although Esther Ahn was just an ordinary girl, the circumstances in which she was raised were anything but ordinary.

The day that Esther was born was a day of great disappointment for her family because she was a girl and not a boy. As Esther's bitter and displeased father held her thin and sickly body in the palm of his hand, somehow he found it within himself to declare, "Poor baby, don't die. But be a great person."

Esther's mother had been introduced to the Jesus of the Bible by American missionaries when she was a young girl, but Esther's father worshipped the Shinto idols. As Esther grew into a young woman, she observed in her mother great joy and peace. However, in her father's side of the family there was a legacy of anger, bitterness and hatred. The dichotomy in which Esther was raised had the power to wound her for life, but Esther chose to nestle into the faith of her mother and so found protection from the rejection and hatred expressed by her father.

Esther was raised in a very dysfunctional family and she could have used her family heritage as an excuse for insecurity and dealing with rejection issues. But Esther was made of the moral fiber that refused to be defined by her family's weaknesses. Have you made that decision? Have you determined that no matter what kind of emotional family lineage you have inherited that you will live well and strong?

Do not use the instability of the previous generations of your family as an excuse for depression and bitterness. You choose how you will live. You cannot choose for the generations past, but you can choose for yourself and your family today.

Joshua, who was chosen to carry on for Moses after his death, had to make the same emotional and spiritual decision. He declared to the children of Israel that it didn't matter how their parents had lived and it mattered even less what choices their culture had made, but that each human being must decide for himself or herself how passionately they would serve the Lord.

"If it is disagreeable in your sight to serve the LORD, choose for yourselves today whom you will serve: whether the gods which your fathers served which were beyond the River, or the gods of the Amorites in whose land you are living; but as for me and my house, we will serve the LORD."

- Joshua 24:15

We cannot afford to waste one day of our lives by agreeing with our culture in its emotional agenda and diatribe. We cannot afford to inherit the pain of generations past and then inflict it upon our children, spouses and friends. We must purpose to serve the Lord wholeheartedly with our spirits and with our souls! This is a crossroads that every woman in all of recorded history must face: *How will I live emotionally? How will I live spiritually?*

Attention!

Esther Ahn Kim's mother had no Bible but remembered four principles taught to her by the American missionaries:

1 - Jesus is the only Son of God and is the only Savior.
2 - Jesus will never forsake His believers.
3 - Jesus is able to take all of our misfortunes and turn them into good.
4 - Jesus hears the prayers of His children.

This simple, 4-pronged theology was written upon Esther's heart as a child and she never forsook the power that she found in the substance of a relationship with Jesus.

In 1939, when Esther was a young music teacher, although she taught in a Christian school, shrine worship was forced upon her. The authorities were going to make sure that everyone in Korea, and especially the Christians, worshiped at the feet of their gods. As Esther made her way up the mountain with her class of girls, Esther purposed in her heart that she would never bow before the idols but only at the feet of Jesus, her Savior.

When Esther made that decision, peace filled her heart and she could barely keep from singing! She was thrilled not to live her youthful life for herself but as a fragrant offering to the Lord. Esther was even joyful that she had been born in such an age of bitterness and conflict.

Esther had to go to the mountain or her principal and perhaps even her students would be tortured. She marched toward her fiery furnace while a civil war raged in her young soul. Would her actions match her words and her strong belief in Jesus Christ?

The scripture that filled Esther's heart and mind and brought a tidal wave of peace to her soul was, *"My sheep hear My voice, and I know them, and they follow Me"* (John 10:27).

"Attention!" The shrill voice on the public address system drilled into Esther's heart. Hundreds of thousands of people straightened line by line, accustomed to enforced subservience. "Our profoundest bow to the sun-goddess!"

As one uninterrupted mass, the enormous crowd of humanity obeyed the shouted order and bowed solemnly and deeply to the caricature of the divine. Only one remained erect with her face looking toward heaven and with her hands reaching toward the sky in worship. Esther Ahn Kim refused to cave into a diabolical and angry culture. She worshipped the God of all creation while others bowed in fear to fiction.

What would you have done that day? We all would like to believe that Esther Ahn's choice would have been our choice, but let's face it, ladies, we can hardly choose to worship the Lord when our husband has gotten on our nerves. When our children are insolent, rather than lovingly train and disciple them, we become the mountain that is exploding with hot lava. When given an opportunity to share our faith, we cower under the basket of embarrassment.

Our emotional choices reveal the strength of our faith and the measure of our love for our Savior. If you have a difficult time choosing joy and kindness when a friend steps on your emotional toes, how would you fare in the culture in which Esther Ahn lived?

Esther was filled with joy that God has chosen her to live during such a difficult hour. Are you filled with joy knowing that God strategically placed challenging people in your life? Are you willing to be used by God when you don't get your way? Is there a song resounding in your heart regardless of your financial state or the condition of your health? Women who have chosen to follow Jesus hear the same music that Esther Ahn Kim heard that day on her way up the torturous mountain.

Prepare for the Worst by Giving Your Best

Because Esther was a teacher, she was considered a leader in her community and was constantly watched by the officials. The military was waiting for her when she returned to her classroom and four burley men led this tiny young lady toward prison. By a miracle of God, she was able to escape from jail and returned to her mother's home.

"The Japanese were crushing untold numbers of believers under their cruel, iron heel in Korea, but actually they had to stand powerless before the Lord. Just as the stars in the sky would not change, God's laws would not change. I wished to shine in the black night sky of my beloved country like a changeless star."

Esther and her mother went into hiding knowing that it was just a matter of time before Esther was once again captured. Her mother prepared her for the torturous rigors of prison and during these days of preparation, Esther memorized hundreds of chapters in the Bible that had been given to her by her sister. She slept without a quilt to prepare herself for the cold and discomfort of prison and ate rotten fruit in order to adjust her digestive system for the sub-standard food that would be fed to her while in confinement. Esther fasted for days at a time to strengthen her resolve that she would live through her time in prison.

Esther was not afraid of dying but was afraid of being tortured and not dying. When Esther Ahn talked with her mother about her fears of prison and the weakness of her soul, her mother responded with this wisdom that is still applicable today, *"It might even be a truer picture of the believer to agonize, to suffer, to be hated and tortured, and even to be killed in obeying God's words rather than to live an ordinary, uneventful life."*

As Esther and her mother hid in the cold, Korean mountains while preparing Esther for what was ahead of her, Esther would often roam the uninhabited rugged wilderness around their borrowed cabin. It was during this time of preparation that Esther Ahn found the strength and joy that comes through singing to the Lord. She sang the great hymns of the faith that thousands had sung before her:

"Did we in our own strength confide, our striving would be losing; Were not the right man on our side, the Man of God's own choosing.

Dost ask who that may be? Christ Jesus it is He, Lord Sabaoth His Name, from age to age the same, and He must win the battle."

(Martin Luther. 1529. "A Mighty Fortress Is Our God." Public domain.)

I have discovered, as did Esther Ahn Kim, that the ability to worship during the worst days of my life is an unconquerable strategy for both spiritual and emotional victory. My friend, when you can't do anything else…you can sing! When you are weakened by the onslaught of people and events…you can sing! When the bills are not paid and the doctor only has bad news…you can still sing! When you are deep in the throes of grief and the mental anxiety is toxic… you can still sing!

The Advanced College of Faith

Esther was imprisoned with 34 other Christians, including a pastor whose faith was unshakable. On the day that Esther was taken to prison, she held her dear mother's hands and looked into her mother's calm, yet radiant face, *"Now I'm going to enter the advanced course in the college of faith. Christ himself is the Principal, so I am sure He will teach me about true faith. Isn't that wonderful?"*

"You must follow Him completely," Esther's mother responded while knowing that she would never see her daughter this side of heaven again. *"If you are to learn from Him, you must lose your life so that Jesus may live within you. That will mean death to yourself every day, every hour, and every minute."*

Dying to self is the healthiest emotional choice you will ever make. Losing your life so that you will be found in Christ is part of the glorious mystery of abundant life. If you maintain the cultural stance of opining self-demands and fulfilling selfish desires, it is the formula for spiritual weakness and emotional sewage. Following Jesus completely embraces the issues of our emotions while living life this side of heaven. He has clearly spelled out the game plan that He has decided is best and it is a strategy of joy and not depression… peace and not confusion…and praise rather than pain. Will you die to self and live for Christ? Living for Christ goes way beyond that miraculous moment when you asked Him into your heart. It is the daily commitment to live in a place of highest praise and exhibit the fruit of His Spirit, never the emotions of self.

Who Lives Like This?!

Esther and her fellow prisoners discovered the joy of the Lord while physically imprisoned in the cesspool of human bitterness and rebellion. Esther's journal recounts the great joy and peace that was found among the Christian prisoners:

> *"We were all filled with the Holy Spirit and were convinced it was more than an honor to die for the Lord. We constantly lived in fear of our guards but we were happy and satisfied, envying no one. Having prayed all night, Pastor would often stand up in joy, dancing and singing, while tears ran down his cheeks."*

Who lives like this? Who has the spiritual tenacity to worship and embrace joy while being tortured by demonic guards? My simple answer to this question is only a woman who has decided to rid herself of emotional residue and subsequently grow a glorious crop of the fruit of the Holy Spirit is able to live like this. Esther Ahn knew a secret that you and I ignore: *When life is at its worst, the Spirit of Christ within us is at Its strongest!* Esther simply made a choice that you and I often refuse: she chose joy when others would justify depression. Esther Ahn Kim chose peace when others would have been tormented by the injustice of imprisonment. This insignificant young woman chose to live a life of significance and power when others would have suffered emotional and mental defeat.

Excrement-caked Lives

Let's read on in Esther Ahn Kim's prison journal: *"It was a joyous blessing to have been born in such a place and for such a time. I realized that it was because of this persecution that I was able to truly experience God's presence where there is fullness of joy!"*

Esther shared a prison cell with seven other Christian women and they spent their waking hours praying, singing and quoting the Word of God to one another. A deranged woman who had lost her mind to mental illness lived in solitary confinement in a cell just down the hallway from the cell shared by the Christian women. This woman had killed her abusive husband and had chopped his body into little pieces before being found. She screamed and yelled shrill profanities all day and all night while the Christians prayed and sang.

One day, Esther Ahn Kim humbly asked the prison guards if they would bring the mad and demented woman to live in her cell with the seven Christian women. The guards were only too happy to do it because they felt that it would be a mocking test for the Christian women.

Esther Ahn held this woman's excrement-caked legs for 72 hours straight so that she would not kill anyone in the tiny prison cell. The women gently ministered to her, wiped her face lovingly and spoke words of endearment and comfort over her tortured soul. At last, when the fog of mental illness lifted, Esther Ahn led this woman to Jesus who then encountered a clarity of mind and will that was nothing short of miraculous.

When this formerly insane woman who was now a vision of peace and joy was led to her persecution, she turned to Esther Ahn Kim and said, "I'll see you at home!"

How are you treating the difficult people in your life? Do you invite them into your home and minister to them? Most of us ignore the difficult people in our lives and when faced with a moment in their presence, we choose to belittle them and unfriend them. The life of Esther Ahn Kim propels me into taking a long, hard look at how I treat the challenging people along life's way. If I am to be a radiant example of estrogen made holy, I must gently minister to these fractious pieces of humanity and show them unconditional love. This is why I am still alive: to reach out in genuine kindness to someone made in the image of God.

Living for a Legacy

Esther Ahn Kim lost most of her sight while in prison and was tortured and beaten too many times to count. Her teeth fell out during her imprisonment and her toes and fingers suffered severe frostbite, but she walked out of prison in 1945 singing, *"All hail the power of Jesus' Name, let angels prostrate fall! Bring forth the royal diadem and crown Him Lord of All!"*
(Edward Perronet. 1779. "All Hail the Power of Jesus' Name." Public domain.)

Will you be remembered for the song of your heart or the screech of your life? We all will leave a legacy that is determined by our daily emotional choices. The emotional and spiritual legacy with which you choose to endow the following generations is more important than the finances, houses or lands that you leave. As you gaze upon the emotional smorgasbord that your culture, your family heritage and your circumstances offer for the substance of your life, never forget that God gives His best to those who leave the choice with Him!

Prayer of Salvation

God loves you—no matter who you are, no matter what your past. God loves you so much that He gave His one and only begotten Son for you. The Bible tells us that "...whoever believes in him shall not perish but have eternal life" (John 3:16 NIV). Jesus laid down His life and rose again so we could spend eternity with Him in heaven and experience His absolute best on earth. If you would like to receive Jesus into your life, say the following prayer out loud and mean it from your heart.

Heavenly Father, I come to You admitting that I am a sinner. Right now, I choose to turn away from sin, and I ask You to cleanse me of all unrighteousness. I believe that Your Son, Jesus, died on the cross to take away my sins. I also believe that He rose again from the dead so that I might be forgiven of my sins and made righteous through faith in Him. I call upon the name of Jesus Christ to be the Savior and Lord of my life. Jesus, I choose to follow You and ask that You fill me with the power of the Holy Spirit. I declare that right now I am a child of God. I am free from sin and full of the righteousness of God. I am saved in Jesus' name. Amen.

If you prayed this prayer to receive Jesus Christ as your Savior for the first time, please contact us on the Web at **harrisonhouse.com** to receive a free book.

Or you may write to us at

Harrison House
P.O. Box 35035
Tulsa, OK 74153

If you are interested in having Carol McLeod speak at your conference or Women's Retreat, please contact us:

Just Joy Ministries
PO Box 252
West Falls, NY 14170

(by phone) 855-569-5433

(by email) info@justjoyministries.com.

For more information, visit our website
at www.JustJoyMinistries.com

Life Changing, Word Driven Books & Teachings by Carol McLeod

Defiant Joy
Rooms of A Woman's Heart
Holy Estrogen
Life Indeed
Who Do You Think You Are
Miracle of Motherhood
Pure Gold
Joy in All Seasons
Hope Scriptures
Healing Scriptures
Joy 150X

All books and CD/DVD teachings are available on the Just Joy website
www.JustJoyMinistries.com

The Harrison House Vision

Proclaiming the truth and the power

Of the Gospel of Jesus Christ

With excellence;

Challenging Christians to

Live victoriously,

Grow spiritually,

Know God intimately.